10 Minute Guide to WordPerfect® 5.1 for Windows™

Debbie Walkowski

A Division of Prentice Hall Computer Publishing
11711 North College, Carmel, Indiana 46032 USA

International Standard Book Number: 0-672-30031-1
Library of Congress Catalog Card Number: 91-61829

95 94 8 7

Interpretation of the printing code: the rightmost double-digit number is the year of the book's first printing; the rightmost single-digit number is the number of the book's printing. For example, a printing code of 92-1 shows that this copy of the book was printed during the first printing of the book in 1992.

Publisher: *Richard K. Swadley*

Associate Publisher: *Marie Butler-Knight*

Publishing Editor: *Marjorie Hopper*

Acquisitions Editor: *Mary-Terese Cozzola-Cagnina*

Development Editor: *Lisa Bucki*

Production Editor: *Elizabeth Keaffaber*

Copy Editor: *Ronda Henry*

Cover Design: *Dan Armstrong*

Indexer: *John Sleeva*

Production Team: *Jeff Baker, Mike Britton, Michelle Cleary, Brook Farling, Joelynn Gifford, Sandy Grieshop, Bob LaRoche, Laurie A. Lee, Matthew Morrill, Mary Beth Wakefield, Corinne Walls, Lisa Wilson*

Special thanks to C. Herbert Feltner for assuring the technical accuracy of this book.

Screen reproductions in this book were created by means of the program Collage Plus from Inner Media, Inc., Hollis, NH.

Printed in the United States of America

Contents

Introduction

Suppose you've just started a new job and your first assignment is to use WordPerfect for Windows to create an important sales proposal. You may be familiar with other word processors, but don't know anything about WordPerfect for Windows.

- You need to learn the program as quickly as possible.
- You need to identify and learn only the most common tasks used to complete your project.
- You need a clear, concise guide that skips the technical jargon and explains tasks in plain English.

You need the *10 Minute Guide to WordPerfect for Windows*.

What Is the 10 Minute Guide?

The *10 Minute Guide* series is a new approach to learning computer programs. Like all *10 Minute Guides,* this one is divided into a series of lessons, each designed to be completed in 10 minutes or less. Each lesson is a self-contained series of steps that teaches you how to perform a task.

The *10 Minute Guide to WordPerfect for Windows* is designed to help you learn the basics of the program as quickly and easily as possible. You'll learn to create files and manipulate text to give your documents a pleasing appearance fast!

Conventions Used in This Book

Each mini-lesson is set up in an easily accessible format. Steps that you must perform are numbered. Pictures of screens appear to show you what to expect. And the following icons appear to provide definitions, warnings, and tips to help you understand what you're doing and how to avoid trouble:

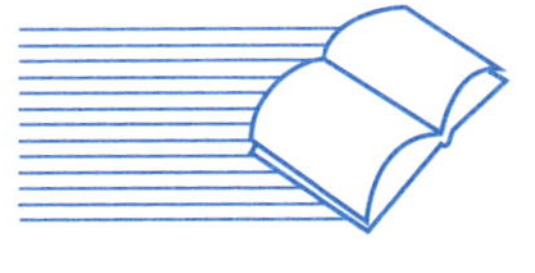

Plain English icons appear wherever a new term is de fined.

Panic Button icons appear where new users commonly run into trouble.

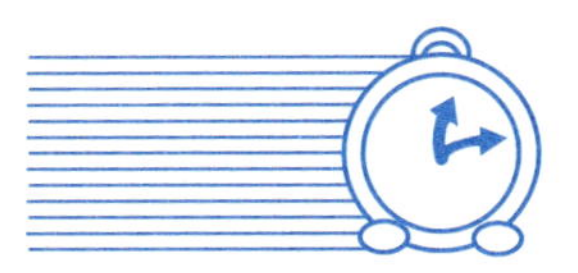

Timesaver Tips offer shortcuts and hints for using the program effectively.

In addition, the following conventions are used to provide a clear idea of what to do:

`What you type`	Information to type appears in color.

Items you select	Any item you select appears in this book's second color. This includes menu and command names, as well as shortcut key combinations. The selection letter for an option appears in bold second color.
`On-screen text`	Any text appearing on-screen is printed in a special monospace font.

Using This Book

If this is your first encounter with a Windows program, read the DOS and Windows Primer at the back of this book. This mini-lesson provides some basic information about DOS (your computer's D isk O perating S ystem) and Windows, your working environment, and how to manage your files, directories and subdirectories. This also includes a Table of Reveal Codes, a Menu Map, and a list of speed keys (listed on the inside back cover).

For Further Reference Consult...

The First Book of WordPerfect for Windows by Kate Barnes

The *10 Minute Guide to Windows* by Katherine Murray

Trademarks

All terms mentioned in this book that are known to be trademarks or service marks are listed below. In addition, terms suspected of being trademarks or service marks have been appropriately capitalized. SAMS cannot attest to the accuracy of this information. Use of a term in this book should not be regarded as affecting the validity of any trademark or service mark.

MS-DOS is a registered trademark of Microsoft Corporation.

Windows is a trademark of Microsoft Corporation.

WordPerfect for Windows is a registered trademark of WordPerfect Corporation.

Lessons

Lesson 1

Getting Started with WordPerfect for Windows

In this lesson, you'll learn how to start and exit WordPerfect for Windows, and you'll become familiar with the WordPerfect for Windows screen.

Starting WordPerfect for Windows

During the installation process, the *WordPerfect for Windows icon* was installed. This icon is necessary for starting the program. Follow these steps to start the program.

If you are using the mouse:

1. If necessary, type `win` at the DOS prompt to start Windows. (If this doesn't work, you need to type `cd\windows` first, then type `win` to start Windows.) When the Windows Program Manager appears, the WordPerfect for Windows icons are displayed in the WordPerfect group.
2. If the Windows Program Manager isn't open, position the mouse pointer on the Program Manager icon and press the left mouse button twice rapidly.

3. If the WordPerfect group window isn't open, position the mouse pointer on the WordPerfect group icon and press the left mouse button twice rapidly.

4. Position the mouse pointer on the WordPerfect icon. Press and release the left mouse button twice quickly.

5. The first time you start WordPerfect for Windows, you'll be asked to enter a license number. You can find your license number printed on the Certificate of License Registration Card that came in your WordPerfect for Windows package. Type the license number in the startup window, then point to the OK button and press the left mouse button once, or just press Enter.

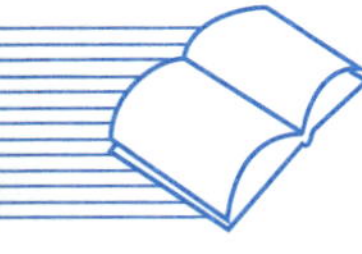

Icon An *icon* is a picture that represents a program (such as WordPerfect for Windows) or a group of programs (such as the Main group under the Windows Program Manager). When you select an icon, it opens a window that either contains more icons, or starts a program.

If you are using the keyboard:

1. If necessary, type `win` at the DOS prompt to start Windows. (If this doesn't work, you need to type `cd/windows` first, then type `win` to start Windows.) When the Windows Program Manager appears, the WordPerfect for Windows icons are displayed in the WordPerfect group.

2. If the Windows Program Manager isn't open, press Alt+Esc until the Program Manager icon is highlighted. Press Ctrl+Esc to display the Task List. Use the up or down arrow to highlight the Program Manager. Press Alt+S.

3. If the WordPerfect group window isn't open in the Program Manager, press Ctrl+F6 until the WordPerfect group icon is highlighted then press Enter.

4. Press the right or left arrow key, if necessary, to highlight the WordPerfect icon, then press Enter to start WordPerfect for Windows.

5. The first time you start the program, you'll be asked to enter a license number. You can find your license number printed on the Certificate of License Registration Card that came in your WordPerfect for Windows package. Type the license number in the startup window, and press Enter.

Feeling Confused? If you haven't installed WordPerfect for Windows yet, see the inside front cover of this book for installation instructions. If you're not completely comfortable working with DOS and Windows, review the DOS and Windows Primer in the back of this book.

Getting Familiar with the Screen

When you start WordPerfect for Windows, a title screen appears briefly, then the document window, shown in Figure 1-1, appears. You'll do most of your work in this window.

The following are some of the components that make up the opening screen.

The *text area* is where you will enter text for your document.

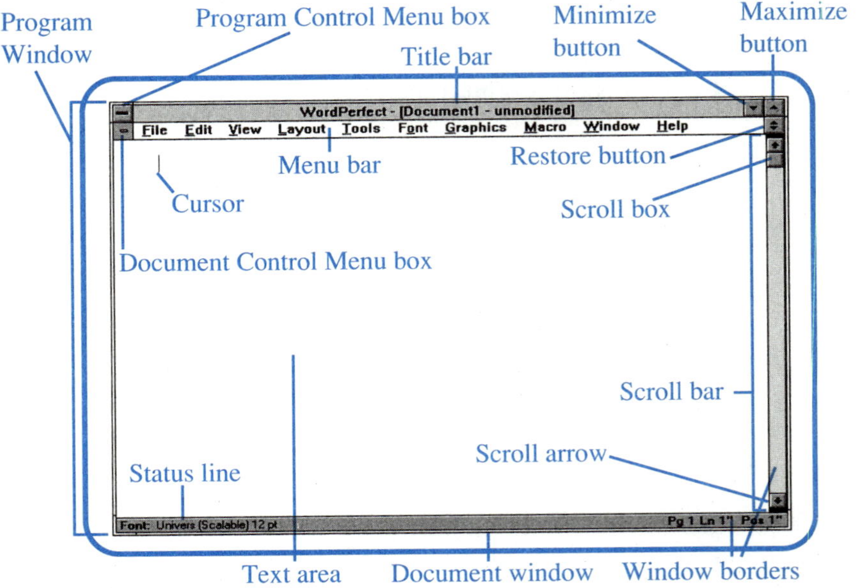

Figure 1-1 The document window.

The *cursor* marks the point where characters are inserted as you type.

The *Title bar* lists the program name (WordPerfect) and the title of your document.

The *Menu* bar lists all of the menu names, each of which contains commands that you learn how to use in Lesson 3.

The *Status line* displays the current font and the current cursor position by page, line, and character position.

There are two *Control Menu boxes*. Both the document and the program Control Menu boxes contain menu commands for closing, restoring, moving, sizing, maximizing, and minimizing the window. However, the program Control Menu box also contains a command for switching to another application, whereas the document Control Menu box contains a command for switching to another document window. (Switching between documents will become important when you learn how to work on more than one document at a time. This is covered in Lesson 22.)

The *Maximize button* enlarges the WordPerfect program window to its maximum size.

The *Minimize button* reduces the WordPerfect program window to its previous size.

The *Restore button* reduces the document window to a size smaller than its maximum size.

The *Borders* are used for resizing a window. Left and right borders resize width, top and bottom resize height, and corner borders resize in two dimensions width and height at once.

The *Scroll bars* allow you to move up and down or right and left through a document. When you click on a *Scroll arrow*, you move through a document in the direction of the arrow. You can click and drag a *Scroll box* to move to an appropriate location in a document.

Using the Button Bar

WordPerfect for Windows offers a *Button Bar* that you may want to add to your WordPerfect for Windows document screen. The Button Bar consists of icons that look like buttons. As you learn to issue commands in WordPerfect for Windows, you will find that "pushing" these buttons with your mouse is a convenient shortcut to the most commonly used menu commands. As you can see in Figure 1-2, the Button Bar has buttons for printing a document, searching for a word, and many other common operations.

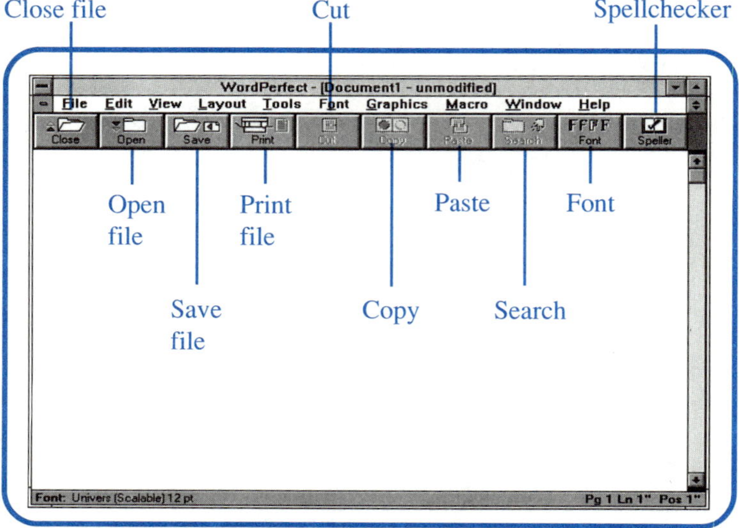

Figure 1-2 The WordPerfect for Windows screen with the Button Bar displayed.

To add the Button Bar to the WordPerfect for Windows screen, use the following steps.

If you are using the mouse:

1. Position the mouse pointer on the View menu and press the left mouse button once.

2. Position the mouse pointer on the Button Bar menu item and press the left mouse button once. The Button Bar appears just below the Menu bar.

If you are using the keyboard:

1. Press Alt.
2. Press V to open the **V**iew menu.
3. Press B to select the Button **B**ar command. The Button Bar appears just below the Menu bar.

Exiting WordPerfect for Windows

Use the following steps to exit WordPerfect for Windows and return to the Windows Program Manager.

If you are using a mouse:

1. Position the mouse pointer on the File menu and press the left mouse button once.
2. When the menu appears, position the mouse pointer on Exit, and press the left mouse button once.

Quick Exit When you use the mouse, you can exit WordPerfect for Windows quickly by positioning the mouse pointer on the Program Control menu box, and pressing the left mouse button twice quickly.

If you are using the keyboard:

1. Press Alt+F to open the **F**ile menu.
2. When the **F**ile menu opens, press X.

Lesson 2

Typing and Moving Around in the Text Area

In this lesson, you'll learn how to enter text, insert blank lines, and move the cursor using the mouse and keyboard.

Entering Text

When you open WordPerfect for Windows, a blank new document window is displayed. You'll notice that most of the space in the document window is devoted to the text area. You begin creating a document simply by typing. The characters you type are inserted to the left of the cursor, which moves along as you type. Try entering text using these steps:

1. Begin typing. When the cursor reaches the end of the first line, just continue typing; WordPerfect for Windows automatically wraps the words you type to the next line.

2. At the end of a paragraph, press Enter to create a *hard return*. The cursor moves to the beginning of the next paragraph.

Hard and Soft Returns Whenever you press Enter to return the cursor to the beginning of the next line, this is known as a *hard return*. When WordPerfect for Windows wraps text at the end of a line, it places a *soft return* at the end of the line. You can learn more about these by referring to Lesson 11, or the Reveal Codes chart at the back of this book.

For practice, type the following text, noting how the words wrap automatically when you reach the end of a line.

```
Perennial Heaven is a nursery that sells a wide
variety of perennial plants through their retail
outlet, located in Redmond, Washington. The
nursery operates as a partnership, and was founded
five years ago by its two current owners.
```

To insert a blank line between paragraphs, press Enter twice at the end of a paragraph. Type the following text as the second paragraph (after the one you just typed).

```
In just five years, Perennial Heaven has become
established as one of the leading perennial
nurseries in western Washington.
```

Typos? For now, don't worry about mistakes you make as you enter text. In Lesson 4, you'll learn how to correct typing errors.

Moving Around the Document Window

Undoubtedly, you'll want to make changes to a document once you have entered text. To make changes, you need to know how to move the cursor within the document. Figure 2-1 illustrates some of the window elements you can use to move around the document window.

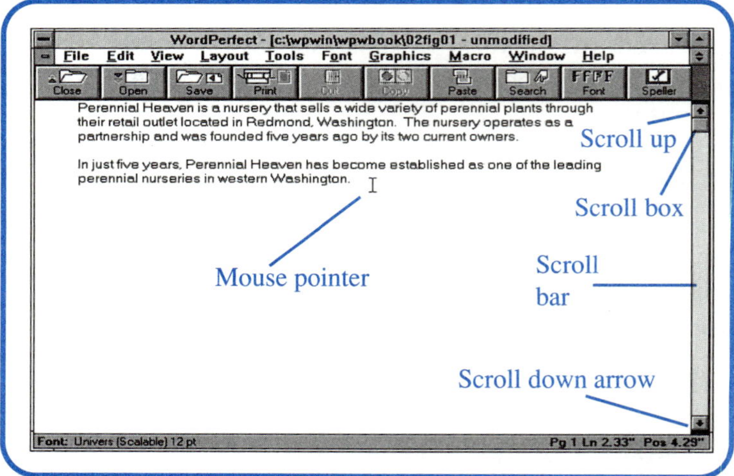

Figure 2-1 Window elements used for moving around the document window.

The mouse pointer changes appearance, depending on where it's located on the screen. When the mouse is located anywhere within the text area of the window, it looks like an *I-beam* (see Figure 2.1).

Once you move the mouse pointer anywhere outside of the text area—into the Button Bar, Menu bar, Status line, or scroll bars—the pointer changes to a *small arrow*.

The rest of this section describes how to use both the keyboard and mouse to move around. Most people, when they become proficient with movement techniques, use both the mouse and keyboard methods.

Moving the Cursor with the Mouse

Using the mouse to move the cursor couldn't be easier. Here's how:

1. Move the mouse until the mouse pointer (the I-beam shown in Figure 2-1) points to the location in the text that you want to move to.

2. Press the left mouse button once. The WordPerfect for Windows cursor moves to the new location.

The basic mouse movement techniques used in the instructions in this book are:

Mouse Technique	Operation
Point	Move the mouse pointer to a specified location on the screen.
Click	Press and release the left mouse button once.
Double-click	Press and release the left mouse button twice quickly.
Click and drag	Press the left mouse button and move the mouse to a new location before releasing the button.

Using a mouse also gives you access to the scroll bars mentioned in Lesson 1 (see Figure 2-1). Use the following techniques to scroll through a document:

Operation	Movement
Click on the up or down scroll arrow, then click inside the text area	To move backward or forward one screen at a time.
Point to either scroll arrow and hold down theleft mouse button , then click inside the text area	To scroll continuously backward or forward.
Drag the scroll box in either direction, then click inside the text area	To move to an approximate location in the document.

Moving the Cursor with the Keyboard

Even if you use a mouse with WordPerfect for Windows, it's helpful to know how to move the cursor with the keyboard. You can use the mouse, the keyboard, or a combination of the two, to move the cursor to a new location. Table 2-1 describes the keys and key combinations used for moving the cursor with the keyboard.

Table 2-1 Keys Used for Moving the Cursor in a Document.

Press	To move the cursor
Up arrow	Up one line
Down arrow	Down one line
Right arrow	Right one character
Left arrow	Left one character
Home	Beginning of the current line
End	End of the current line
Ctrl+Home	Beginning of the document
Ctrl+End	End of the document
Ctrl+up arrow	Beginning of the current or previous paragraph
Ctrl+down arrow	Beginning of the next paragraph
Ctrl+right arrow	Beginning of the next word
Ctrl+left arrow	Beginning of the current or previous word

Lesson 3

Working with Menus and Dialog Boxes

In this lesson, you'll learn how to work with WordPerfect for Windows' menus and dialog boxes, issue commands using the mouse and the keyboard, and get help when you need it.

How the Menus Work

In WordPerfect for Windows, you issue a command to tell WordPerfect what you want it to do. Commands are listed on menus. The menu names appear on the WordPerfect for Windows Menu bar. When you select a menu, it opens up or *pulls down* to reveal a list of commands like those shown in Figure 3-1.

Each menu name and command has an underlined selection letter. Menu commands that toggle on and off display a check mark next to the command name when selected. Menu commands that are followed by a *right arrow* display a *submenu* when you select them. A submenu gives you more specific choices for the menu command. Figure 3-1 also illustrates a submenu for the **J**ustification command on the Layout menu. This submenu allows you to choose **L**eft, **R**ight, Center, or **F**ull justification.

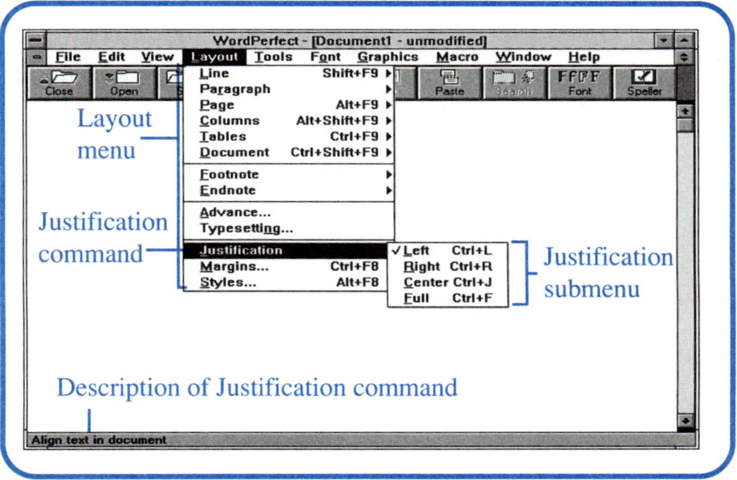

Figure 3-1 The submenu for the Justification command on the Layout menu.

When you select a menu name or menu command, WordPerfect for Windows displays a brief description of the menu or command on the Status line. You can see an example of this in Figure 3-1. In Figure 3-1, WordPerfect says the **J**ustification command is used to "align text in document." This is a handy feature to keep in mind when you're not sure what a menu or a specific command is used for.

Using the Mouse to Select Menu Commands

You can select menus and menu commands using either the mouse or the keyboard. To use the mouse, follow these steps:

1. Point to the menu name, then click.
2. When the menu opens, point to the command you want to select, then click.
3. If the command opens a submenu, point to the command you want to select, then click.

Using the Keyboard to Select Menu Commands

Follow these steps to select menus and commands using the keyboard.

1. Press Alt.
2. Press the selection letter (underlined on the screen, bold in this book) in the name of the menu you want to choose.
3. When the menu opens, press the selection letter for the command you want to choose.
4. If the command opens a submenu, type the selection letter for the command you want to choose.

For some commands, WordPerfect for Windows uses *speed keys* to let you select the command quickly. A speed key is usually one key or two keys pressed in sequence. For example, to print a document, you can press F5, and to exit WordPerfect for Windows, you can press Alt+F4. You don't have to learn or memorize these speed keys; they are displayed to the right of the command on the menu. (Note that all commands don't have speed keys.) Speed keys are pointed out throughout this book where applicable.

Choose the Wrong Menu? You can escape from any menu by clicking the mouse pointer anywhere outside the menu, or by pressing Esc until the menu disappears.

Throughout this book, you'll see instructions that tell you to "select X," as in "Select the Print command on the **F**ile menu." You can use either the mouse or the keyboard method to select menus and menu commands.

Working with Dialog Boxes

Menu commands that are followed by an *ellipsis (...)* open a *dialog box*. A dialog box is a separate window that asks you to give more specific information about the command you have chosen. For example, if you select the **M**argins command on the **L**ayout menu shown in Figure 3-1, the dialog box that is displayed allows you to specify the exact width for the **l**eft, **r**ight, **t**op, and **b**ottom margins.

Before you select a command that displays a dialog box, you need to understand the different elements used in dialog boxes. Table 3-1 shows common dialog box elements, and how to work with them. The Open File dialog box, shown in Figure 3-2, includes four dialog box elements: the text box, the list box, the check box, and command buttons.

Table 3-1 Dialog Box Elements and How to Work with Them.

Element	Use
Text boxes	Type in the information you are asked for.
List boxes	Select one item in the list. Use the scroll bar, if necessary, to display all items in the list.
Check boxes	Turn the associated options on and off each time you select one. You can choose more than one check box when multiple check boxes are displayed.
Command buttons	Select the button to activate a command, such as OK or Cancel.
Option buttons	Although multiple option buttons may appear in a dialog box, you may choose only one in each group (see Figure 3-3).

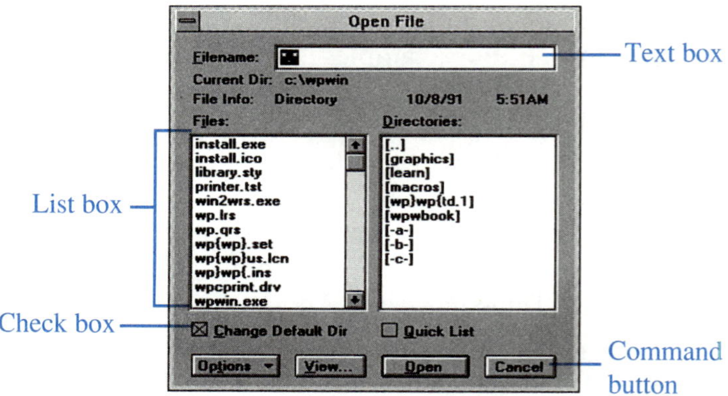

Figure 3-2 The Open File dialog box.

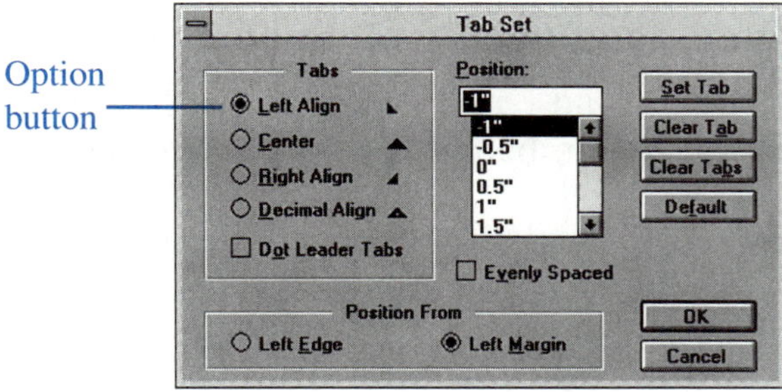

Figure 3-3 The Tab Set dialog box.

Occasionally, text boxes and other dialog box elements have a pull-down (upward-pointing and downward-pointing) arrow. These are used either to choose from a list of suggested entries, or to change a number in a box instead of typing a new entry.

Making selections in a dialog box is easy. Just use one of the following procedures.

If you are using a mouse:

1. Click on the dialog box option you want. For the text box, click on the box and then enter the appropriate text.
2. When all settings are correct, select the OK button to confirm the settings and close to the dialog box.

If you are using a keyboard, make your selections by following these techniques:

- *Text boxes*: Select the box, then type an entry. (Note that to move to another option from a text box, you must press Alt, then a selection letter.)

- *List boxes*: Type the selection letter, then use the up and down arrow keys to select an entry.

- *Option buttons* and *check boxes*: Type the selection letter for the option button or check box you want to select.

- *Pull-down list boxes*: Type the selection letter, press the down arrow to display the list, then type the selection letter.

- *Command buttons*: Type the selection letter. When there is no selection letter, press Tab until the button is selected, then press Enter.

Dialog Box Mistakes? All dialog boxes have a Cancel button that lets you return to the document window without making any changes in the dialog box.

Getting Help

WordPerfect for Windows provides extensive on-line help. Through the **H**elp menu, you can choose one of the following help topics:

Topic	Function
Index	An alphabetic list of help topics to choose from.
Keyboard	Instructions on how to use the keyboard and what specific keys are for.

Topic	Function
How Do I	A list of the most common WordPerfect for Windows tasks with explanations for how to perform them.
Glossary	An alphabetic list of terms used in WordPerfect for Windows.
What Is	Displays a *question mark thought bubble* in place of the mouse pointer. Move the thought bubble to any menu name or menu command and click it on for an explanation of the menu itself or the command.

When you select any of the Help commands on the **H**elp menu, WordPerfect for Windows displays a separate Help window. At the top of the help window are the following command buttons.

Command button	Operation
Index	Displays the same list of topics shown when you select the Index command from the Help menu.
Back	Displays the last help topic you looked at.
Browse <<	Moves backwards through a series of related topics.
Browse >>	Moves forward through a series of related topics.

Search	Lists all help keywords, which you can select to move directly to that help topic.

Selecting a Help Topic

To select a help topic, follow these steps.

1. Select the Help menu.
2. Select a help topic from the menu.
3. When the Help window appears, scroll through the information in the window or use the command buttons at the top of the window to find the information you want.

Getting Help As You Work

As you're working, you can get help on the specific task you're doing or on any menu command by pressing F1. If you want to use the What Is thought bubble as you're working, follow these steps.

1. As you're working, press Shift+F1 or select the What Is command on the Help menu.
2. To get help on a menu or menu command, click and hold down the mouse button while you make your selection. The item at which you are pointing when you release the mouse button is the item on which you'll get help.

Lesson 4

Editing Your Text

In this lesson, you'll learn how to insert and type over text, and correct minor typing errors.

Adding Text to Your Documents

WordPerfect for Windows offers two different ways to enter text. You can *insert* text in a document, or you can *type over* existing text that you want to change. You'll find both modes useful depending on the type of work you're doing—and you can switch between modes easily.

Inserting Text

Inserting text means adding text *between* existing text in a document. For example, you might insert a word in a sentence or insert a new sentence in a paragraph. When you insert text, WordPerfect for Windows automatically moves existing text to the right, to make room for the new text you type. You can insert text anywhere in a WordPerfect for Windows document.

The Default WordPerfect for Windows is always in *Insert* mode unless you change to *Typeover* mode, which you'll learn about later in this lesson.

Use the following steps to insert text into a document.

1. Move the cursor to the point where you want to begin inserting text.
2. Begin typing. If you're inserting a paragraph, press Enter twice at the end of the paragraph to add a blank line.

In the document shown in Figure 4-1, a sentence was inserted by placing the cursor to the left of the "T" in "The" at the beginning of the last sentence. The two paragraph headings were inserted by moving the cursor to the beginning of each paragraph, entering the headings, and then pressing Enter twice.

Typing Over Existing Text

Sometimes it's easier and faster to type over a word or a sentence rather than deleting and retyping it. You can type over existing characters while WordPerfect for Windows is in *Typeover* mode, as follows:

1. Place the cursor at the point where you want to begin typing over text.
2. Press Insert. The Status line now says "Typeover," indicating that WordPerfect is in Typeover mode.

3. Begin typing the new text. Each new character you type replaces the old.

4. When you reach the end of the text you want to replace, press Insert again to return to Insert mode.

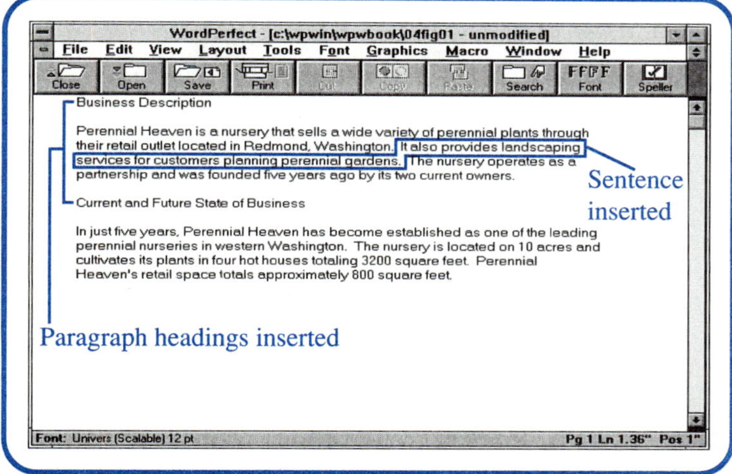

Figure 4-1 The sample document with a sentence and two headings inserted.

Returning to Insert Mode In Typeover mode, the character at the cursor position is overwritten by the new character you type. Once Typeover mode is selected, WordPerfect for Windows remains in Typeover mode until you switch back to Insert mode, by pressing Insert again.

Correcting Minor Errors

In WordPerfect for Windows, you can correct errors in a number of different ways using the mouse, keyboard, or a combination of the two. The method you choose usually depends on the amount of text you're deleting.

To delete one character or a few characters at a time:

- Press Backspace to delete one character at a time to the left of the cursor.
- Press Delete to delete one character at a time to the right of the cursor.

Getting Rid of Text Quickly You can delete characters continuously by pressing and holding Backspace and Delete. When using this method, the cursor moves very quickly, so watch your screen carefully to avoid deleting too much text.

To delete one word at a time, follow these steps:

1. Move the cursor to any character in the word you want to delete.
2. Press Ctrl+Backspace. WordPerfect for Windows deletes the current word and the space following it.

To delete the remainder of the current line—that is, everything from the point of the cursor to the end of the line—follow these steps.

1. Move the cursor to the point where you want to begin deleting.

2. Press Ctrl+Delete. All text from the cursor position to the end of the line is deleted.

Lesson 5

Selecting Text Blocks

In this lesson, you'll learn how to select blocks of text using the mouse and the keyboard.

What Is a Text Block?

A *text block* is any amount of text that you want to work with—it can be as small as one character or as large as an entire document. In WordPerfect for Windows, you select text blocks when you want to make a change to the entire block. For example, you might want to delete a sentence, move or copy a phrase, underline a title, or change the margins used to format a paragraph.

When you select text, you are telling WordPerfect for Windows which text you want to modify in the next procedure. In Figure 5-1, the second paragraph is selected. Notice that the Status line reads "Select On" and the selected text is highlighted on the screen.

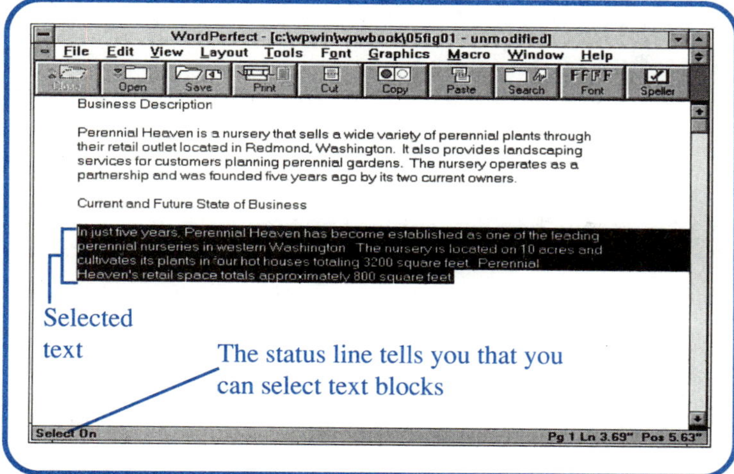

Figure 5-1 WordPerfect for Windows highlights selected text on your screen.

Selecting Text Blocks with the Mouse

Selecting text using the mouse couldn't be easier. Follow these steps:

1. Point to the first letter of the text block you want to select.
2. Press and hold the left mouse button while you drag the mouse to the last character of the text you want to modify. The area of highlighted text grows as you drag.
3. Release the mouse button. WordPerfect for Windows highlights the selected text.

Practice these steps—point, press, drag, and release—to select a word, phrase, or sentence using the mouse.

Selecting Text Blocks Using the Keyboard

To select text using the keyboard, follow these steps:

1. Point to the first letter of the text block you want to select.
2. Press F8. The "Select Mode" message appears on the Status line.
3. Press any of the following keys or key combinations to select text.
   - Right or left arrow to select one or more characters at a time.
   - Ctrl+Shift+right arrow to select one word at a time to the right of the cursor.
   - Ctrl+Shift+left arrow to select one word at a time to the left of the cursor
   - Down or up arrow to select from the current cursor position to the same cursor position one line down or up.
4. WordPerfect for Windows highlights the selected text on the screen.

Select the Wrong Text? Click anywhere in the window or press F8 to cancel the selection.

Lesson 6

Deleting, Moving, and Copying Blocks of Text

In this lesson, you will learn how to delete blocks of text, as well as rearrange text using the move and copy features.

Deleting Text

In Lesson 4, you learned how to delete small amounts of text using Backspace and Delete. When you want to delete large amounts of text, it's more efficient to select the text first, then delete it. To delete a block of text, follow these steps:

1. Select the text you want to delete, including tabs, spaces, and blank lines. The "Select On" indicator appears on the Status line. WordPerfect for Windows highlights the selected text.

2. Press Delete. The selected text is removed.

Select the Wrong Text? Just click anywhere in the document area or press F8 to cancel the selection. If you delete the wrong text, see the next section in this lesson, "Undeleting Text."

Undeleting Text

There will be times when you delete something accidentally—it happens! But don't worry, all is not lost. WordPerfect for Windows has a command that brings back deleted text: *Undo*. There are two important things to remember about the **U**ndo command:

- You must use **U**ndo *immediately* before doing any other type of editing, including entering new text.
- You can only bring back the most *recently deleted text*. If you select text and press Delete several times, you can only recover the text from the last delete.

To bring back deleted text:

- Immediately after deleting text, select the Undo command on the **E**dit menu.

  Or,

- Immediately after deleting text, press Alt+Backspace.

Moving Text

One of the great advantages of using a word processing program is that you can continue to change a document until it's perfect—and moving text is something you might need to do frequently. When you move text, it is removed from the document and placed into the Windows *Clipboard.* The Clipboard is a temporary storage area from which you can move the text to another location in the document, to another document, or to another Windows application. Here's how to move text:

1. Select the text you want to move.
2. Select the Cut command on the **E**dit menu or select Cut on the Button Bar. The selected text is removed from the document and placed in the Clipboard.
3. Place the cursor at the location you want to move the text to.
4. Select the Paste command on the **E**dit menu or select Paste on the Button Bar.

Cut and Paste Shortcuts In place of the Cut command, press Shift+Delete, and in place of the Paste command, press Shift+Insert.

In Figure 6-1, the heading "Business Description" and the accompanying paragraph are selected to be moved below the second heading and paragraph, "Current and Future State of Business." The selected text and the cursor location the text is to be moved to are pointed out in the figure.

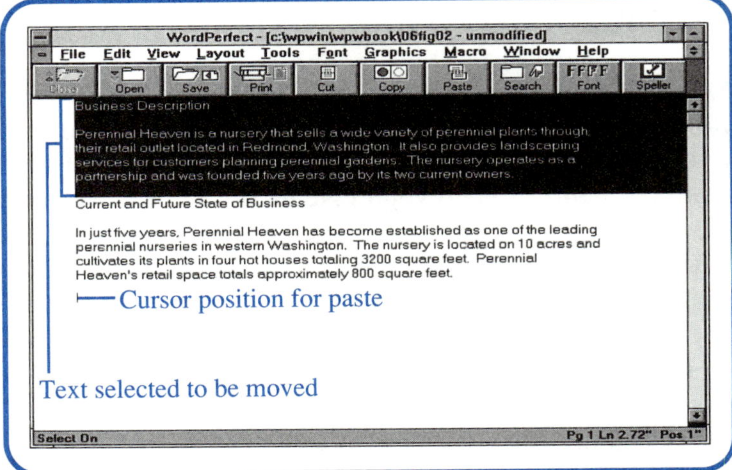

Figure 6-1 The text is selected for moving to another location in the document.

Figure 6-2 illustrates how the document looks after the selected text is moved.

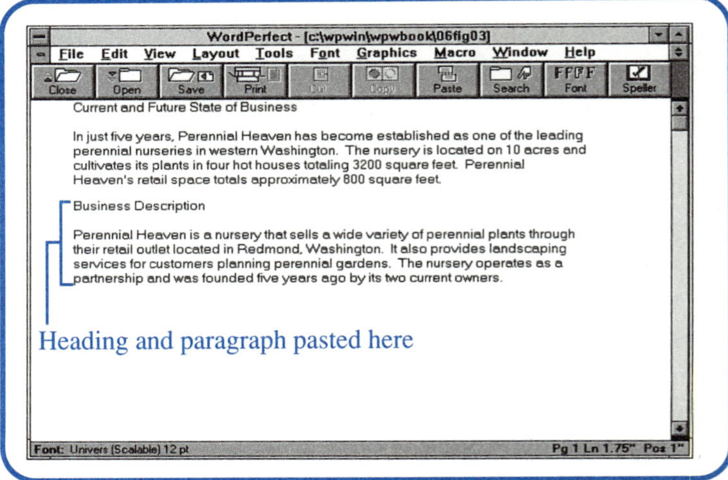

Figure 6-2 The selected text has been moved to the new location.

Copying Text

When you use the Copy command, WordPerfect for Windows puts a copy of the text you select into the Windows Clipboard. Just like when you move text, you can copy text from the Clipboard to another location in the same document, to another document, or to a Windows application. These steps tell you how to copy the selected text to another location within the same document.

1. Select the text you want to copy.
2. Select the Copy command on the Edit menu or select Copy on the Button Bar. The selected text remains in the document and a copy is placed in the Clipboard.
3. Move the cursor to the location where you want the text to be copied.
4. Select the Paste command on the Edit menu or select Paste on the Button Bar. WordPerfect for Windows copies the text from the Clipboard to the new location.

Copy and Paste Shortcuts In place of the **C**opy command, press Ctrl+Ins, and in place of the **P**aste command, press Shift+Insert.

Because the text you select is placed in the Clipboard, you can use the steps above to copy the text to more than one location if you wish. The text remains in the Clipboard until you use the Cu**t** or **C**opy command again, which removes the old text and places new text into the Clipboard.

Lesson 7

Saving a Document

In this lesson, you'll learn how to name and save WordPerfect for Windows documents.

Naming a Document

When you create a new document, WordPerfect for Windows temporarily names it `document*` (the asterisk is a number WordPerfect for Windows assigns). This file name is displayed in the Title bar. When you're ready to save a document, you can store it on the hard disk or on a floppy disk. At this point, you must assign the file a permanent file name.

In WordPerfect for Windows, the file name you choose can be up to eight characters long. The name can be any combination of letters or numbers, or both, but it may not include any of the following characters:

, * + = [ ] ; : “ ? < > \ / | space

If you like, you may add a *file extension* following the file name. File extensions are used to categorize files, usually by file type. They begin with a period and are up to three characters long. For example, you might save all the letters you create with the .ltr file extension, as in budget.ltr.

The Save Commands

WordPerfect for Windows has two Save commands: **S**ave and Save **A**s. The *Save As* command displays the Save **A**s dialog box, which allows you to specify a file name for your document and choose the directory in which you want the file stored. The *Save* command doesn't display a dialog box; it just saves your document under the same name and the same directory it was last saved. The exception to this is if you choose the **S**ave command the first time you save a new document. In this case, the Save **A**s dialog box is displayed so you can name the file.

In the Save As dialog box, shown in Figure 7-1, the current directory is displayed just below the Save **A**s text box. Unless you specify otherwise, the directory in which all WordPerfect for Windows files are stored is `c:\wpwin`. The files currently stored in this directory are shown in the Files list box. Other directories on your computer are shown in the Directories list box.

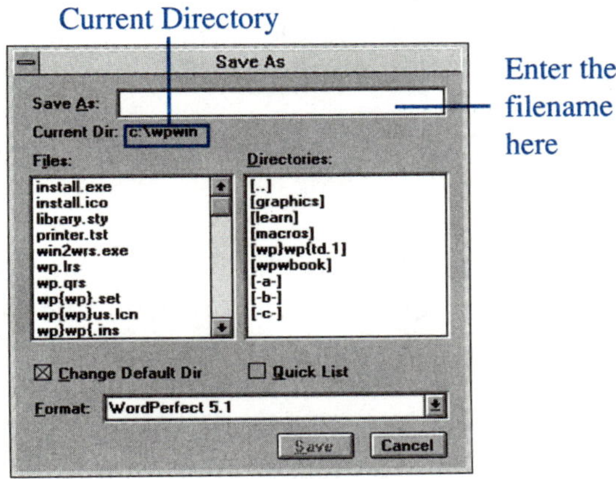

Figure 7-1 The Save As dialog box.

Directories A directory is a a section on the hard drive where files are stored. You can create a directory to help you keep your files organized.

Confused About Files and Directories? See the DOS and Windows Primer at the back of this book.

Saving a New Document

Before you can save a new document, you must give it a name. You can use either the Save or Save As command to do this, because the first time you save a document, WordPerfect for Windows automatically displays the Save As dialog box. Use the following steps to save your new document.

1. Select either the Save or the Save As command on the File menu (or, press Shift+F3). WordPerfect for Windows displays the Save As dialog box shown in Figure 7-1.

2. Enter a file name for the document in the Save As text box.

3. If you want to store the file in a directory other than `c:\wpwin`, select a directory from the Directories list box.

4. Select Save. WordPerfect for Windows saves your file and continues to display it on your screen in the document window.

Saving Again

Once you have named and saved a new document, it becomes an *existing* document. You may work on an existing document many times before it is complete, and you will probably want to save subsequent versions. If you want to save the document under the same name and directory, use the Save command. Choose one of these methods:

- Select the Save command on the **F**ile menu.
- Press Shift+F3.
- Click on the Save button on the Button Bar.

Remember, you won't see a dialog box, but the Status line displays a message that the document is being saved.

You can tell WordPerfect to automatically create a backup copy of your file each time you save a document. The file is saved with a .bak file extension. Follow these steps:

1. Select the Preferences command on the **F**ile menu.
2. Select the **B**ackup command to display the Backup dialog box.
3. Select the **O**riginal Document Backup check box.
4. Specify the number of minutes between backups in the text box.
5. Select OK.

If you prefer to have WordPerfect create a backup copy only in the case of a power failure, select the Timed Document Backup check box instead of the Original Document Backup check box in Step 3.

The previous steps save only the version of the document that you're editing. If you are editing a document for the fifth time, Original Document Backup saves only the fourth and fifth version; the fifth version is saved under the file name you give it. If you want to save every version of a document, use the Save As command and rename the file each time you save it. For instance, if your document is called report.doc, you might save subsequent versions as report2.doc, report3.doc, and so on.

Saving As You Work

Whether you are entering text in a new document or making changes to an existing one, none of your work is stored on your computer's hard disk or a floppy disk until you save it. So, it's a good idea to get into the habit of saving a document as you work. If you're making extensive changes, that could mean saving a document every five or ten minutes or so. Saving a document frequently is important, because if the power to your computer is interrupted for any reason, you'll lose the changes you have made since the last time you saved the document. All it takes is a surge of electricity, a power failure, or a trip over the power cord! Make it a habit to save your work regularly.

Lesson 8

Previewing and Printing a Document

In this lesson, you'll learn how to preview a document on-screen and print it when you're ready.

Previewing a Document

The *preview* feature of WordPerfect for Windows lets you see on-screen how your document will look when it's printed. This feature is helpful for checking the layout of a document from page to page. It is also especially helpful for viewing some of the elements you add to a document that are not visible in the document window, such as headers and footers. (You'll learn how to create headers and footers in Lesson 18.) Use the following steps to preview a document.

1. With the document displayed in the document window, select the Print Preview command from the **F**ile menu or press Shift+F5. WordPerfect for Windows displays your document in the Print Preview window, as shown in Figure 8-1.

2. You can move through the document using the scroll bars, Page Up, Page Down, or the arrow keys.

3. When you are finished previewing the document, select the Close command on the **F**ile menu, or select the Close button on the Button Bar to close the Preview window, and return to the document window.

Preview Shortcut Use Shift+F5 in place of the Print Preview command to display the preview window.

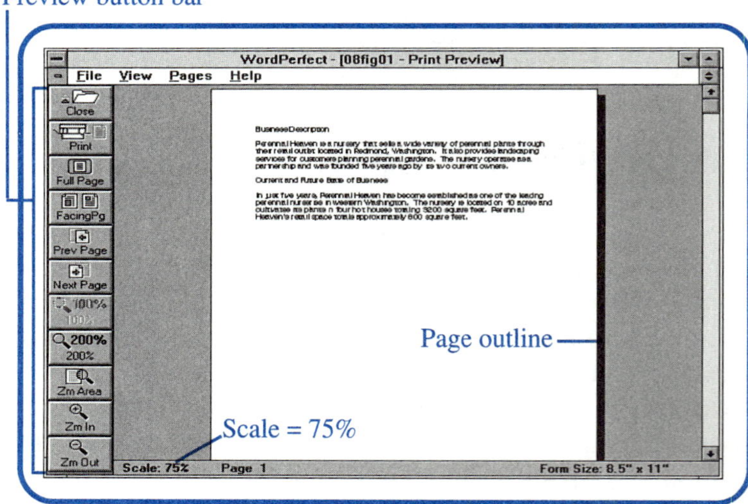

Figure 8-1 The Print Preview screen displaying a page at 75% scale.

Because most personal computer monitors are not large enough to display an entire page on-screen, WordPerfect for Windows reduces the page shown. The actual size displayed may depend on the type and resolution of your computer's monitor. For example, the Print Preview command may display your document at 75% of its actual size (see Figure 8-1).

Whatever the actual size displayed, the Status bar tells you the scale you are currently viewing. When the Status bar reads 100%, the text is displayed at the actual size it will be printed. The document shown in Figure 8-2 is displayed at 100%.

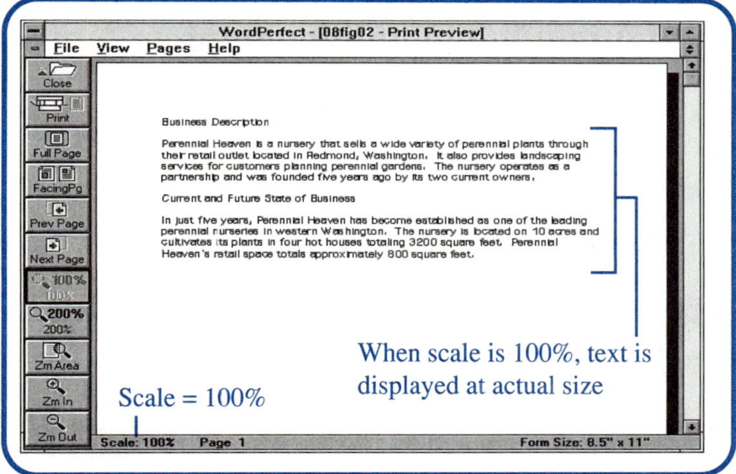

Figure 8-2 The Print Preview screen displaying a page at 100%.

Altering the View of a Document

At certain percentages (again, depending on the type and resolution of your monitor), the text on the Preview screen may become unreadable. This may be acceptable if you are using Preview just to check the layout of a document. If not, you can make the text readable by enlarging the view. Try using some of the following commands on the **V**iew menu or the Preview Button Bar to change the view of the document.

Command	**Function**
100%	Displays the text at its actual size when printed.
200%	Displays the text at twice its actual size when printed.
Zoom In	Magnifies the current size by 25% each time you select this command. You can zoom in up to 400%.
Zoom Out	Reduces the current size by 25% each time you choose this command.
Zoom Area	Chooses a specific area on the page to enlarge.
Zoom to Full Width	Views the full width of the current page.

In addition to the viewing options just described, you can view more than one page at a time by using the following commands on the Pages menu.

Command	**Function**
Full Page	Displays a full-page view of the current page.
Facing Pages	Displays two consecutive pages side by side. Odd pages are shown on the right, and even pages on the left.

Revising a Document

If you find errors in your document when previewing it, you must return to the document window to correct them; you can't edit in the Preview window. Select the Close command on the File menu, or select the Close button in the Button Bar to return to the document window.

Printing a Document

Once you have previewed a document, you're ready to print. Use the following steps to print a document.

1. Make sure your printer is turned on and is ready to print.
2. With the document you want to print displayed in the document window, select the **Print** command on the **F**ile menu, or press F5. WordPerfect for Windows displays the Print dialog box shown in Figure 8-3.
3. The Current Printer box displays the printer name that's currently selected. If you want to select a different printer, choose the Select button, which displays the Select Printers dialog box. Select a printer from the **A**vailable Printers list box, then choose the Select button. WordPerfect returns to the Print dialog box.
4. If you want to print more than one copy, enter the number in the Number of Copies box.
5. If your printer is capable of printing at different qualities (that is, different speeds) you can choose the quality in the Text Quality box.
6. When all settings are correct, select **Print**.

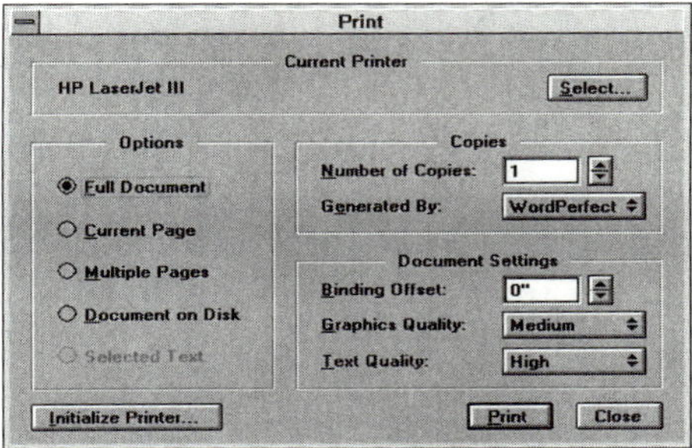

Figure 8-3 The Print dialog box.

Quick Pick You can display the Print dialog box instantly by selecting the Print button on the Button Bar.

If you use Print Preview, you also have the option of printing directly from that point. If everything in the document looks correct in the preview window, you can select the Print button and follow steps 3 through 6 (explained earlier) to select print settings and print the document.

Lesson 9

Retrieving and Finding a Document

In this lesson, you'll learn how to find and retrieve a document previously saved, so you can work on it again.

Retrieving an Existing Document

Retrieving a document is easy when you know the name, and you saved the file in the WordPerfect for Windows default directory, `c:\wpwin`. To see why, let's look at the Retrieve File dialog box shown in Figure 9-1. This dialog box is displayed when you select the **R**etrieve command on the **F**ile menu.

Retrieve vs. Open **R**etrieve opens a file in the active window; **O**pen opens a file in a new document window. To learn how to use the **O**pen command, see Lesson 22.

In Figure 9-1, you can see that WordPerfect for Windows automatically goes to the `c:\wpwin` directory when you select the **R**etrieve command. All the files listed in the F**i**les list box are stored in this directory. Unless you saved your file under a different directory, the file name is listed in the Files box. Use the following steps to retrieve a document.

1. Select the **R**etrieve command on the **F**ile menu. WordPerfect for Windows displays the Retrieve File dialog box.

2. Select a file name from the F**i**les list box.

3. Select the **R**etrieve button. WordPerfect for Windows retrieves the file to the active window.

When the file you want is stored in a directory other than `c:\wpwin`, follow these steps to retrieve the file:

1. Select the **R**etrieve command on the **F**ile menu. WordPerfect for Windows displays the Retrieve File dialog box.

2. Select the correct directory from the **D**irectories list. The files shown in the F**i**les box are updated to reflect the new directory you choose.

3. Select a file name from the F**i**les list box.

4. Select the **R**etrieve button. WordPerfect for Windows retrieves the file to the active window.

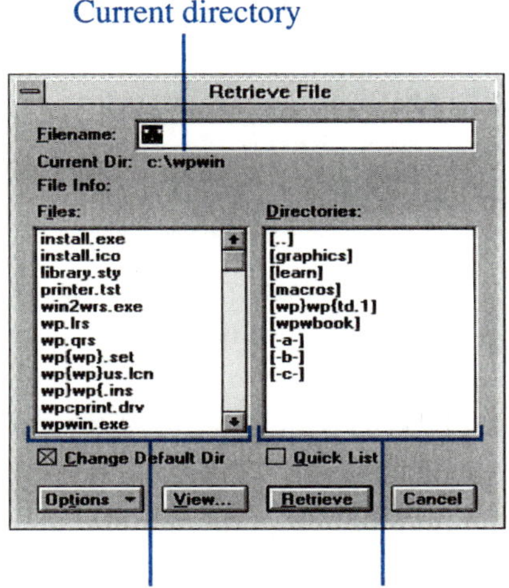

Figure 9-1 The Retrieve File dialog box.

Backing Up You can move backwards in the directory hierarchy by selecting the [..] symbol. For example, when the current directory is c:\wpwin, selecting the [..] symbol changes the current directory to c:\. If you need more information about directories, see the DOS and Windows primer at the end of the book.

Changing the Default Directory

As you learned earlier in this lesson, WordPerfect for Windows automatically saves all files to the directory `c:\wpwin`; therefore, it automatically retrieves files from this directory as well, unless you change it. If you routinely store your files in a different directory, you can have

WordPerfect for Windows automatically go to that directory when you use the **R**etrieve command. Try these steps to change your default retrieval directory.

1. Select the **R**etrieve command on the **F**ile menu.
2. From the Directories box, select the directory you want to use as the default directory.
3. Select the Change Default Dir check box.
4. Select the Cancel button. The next time you use the **R**etrieve command, WordPerfect for Windows automatically displays the files in the directory you chose.

Finding the Document to Retrieve

When you know the name of a file, but you're not sure which directory you stored it, you can find it using the Find feature in the Retrieve File dialog box. Here's how.

1. Select the **R**etrieve command on the **F**ile menu. WordPerfect for Windows displays the Retrieve File dialog box.
2. Select the Options button. When the pull-down menu appears, select the Find command. WordPerfect for Windows displays the Find dialog box shown in Figure 9-2.
3. Select the Find Files button. WordPerfect for Windows displays the Find Files dialog box shown in Figure 9-3.

4. In the File Pattern text box, type the name of the file to find. (If you are looking for a file on a floppy disk, type the drive name, a semicolon and the file name.)

5. In the Apply Find to Current box, select **D**irectory, **S**ubtree, **D**rive, or **S**earch Results **L**ist, then select the **F**ind button. In the search, WordPerfect for Windows finds all files you specified that match the file name you entered. The files are listed in the Search Results area of the dialog box. (Choose **D**rive if you are looking for a file on a floppy disk.)

6. Select a file from the list, then select the **R**etrieve button. The file is retrieved to the active window.

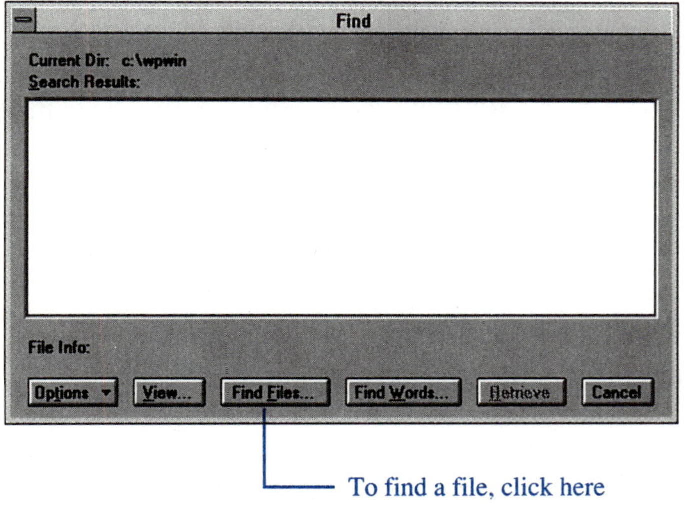

Figure 9-2 The Find dialog box.

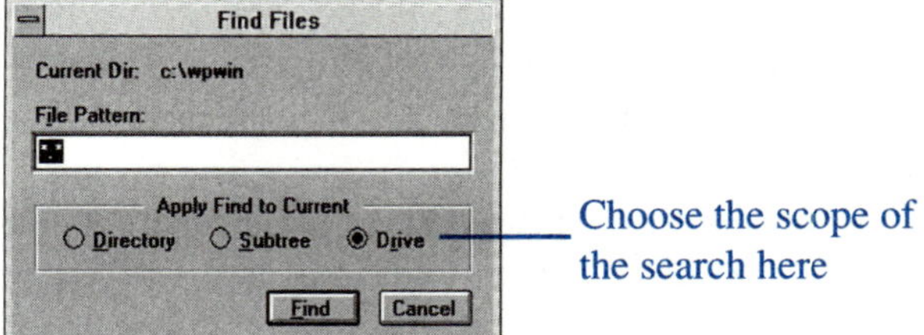

Figure 9-3 The Find Files dialog box.

Viewing a File Before Retrieving

When you're not sure whether the file you have chosen to retrieve is the right file, you can view a sample of the file without actually retrieving it. Here's how:

1. Select the **R**etrieve command on the **F**ile menu. WordPerfect for Windows displays the Retrieve File dialog box.
2. Select a file name from the F**i**les list box.
3. Select the **V**iew button. WordPerfect for Windows displays a portion of the file you selected in a separate View window.
4. If the file shown is correct, select the Retrieve button to retrieve the file. If the file is not correct, you may select another file to display in the View window.
5. Select Cancel to close the Retrieve File dialog box and return to the document window.

Lesson 10
Enhancing Text

In this lesson, you'll learn how to enhance text by using features, such as boldface, italic, and underline.

Understanding Text Enhancements

A *text enhancement* is a characteristic, such as underlining, that you use to add emphasis to plain text.

The most common text enhancements are boldface, italic, and underline, but WordPerfect for Windows offers additional enhancements, described in Table 10-1. These commands toggle on and off each time you select them. When an enhancement is active, a check mark appears beside the command name.

Table 10-1 WordPerfect for Windows Character Enhancements.

Enhancement	Description
Normal	Restores enhanced character to unenhanced
Bold	Displays and prints character in heavier print
Underline	Displays and prints character with an underline beneath it

continues

Table 10-1 continued

Enhancement	Description
Double Underline	Displays and prints character with two underlines beneath it
Italic	Displays and prints character in an italic (slanted) font
Outline	Outlines each character
Shadow	Shades each character to give the appearance of being shadowed
Small Cap	Changes a lowercase character to a small uppercase character
Redline	On a color monitor, displays character in red; when printed on noncolor printer, display character with shaded background
Strikeout	Displays and prints character with a line drawn through horizontally

There are two methods for enhancing text in WordPerfect for Windows:

- Applying enhancements as you enter new text.
- Applying enhancements after the text has been entered, by selecting a block of text.

You can use either method to apply text enhancements to selected portions of your document. The following sections describe both procedures in more detail.

Enhancing Text as You Type

Commands for the **N**ormal, **B**old, **U**nderline, **D**ouble Underline, **I**talic, **R**edline, and Stri**k**eout enhancements appear on the F**o**nt menu. To use any of these enhancements, follow these steps:

1. Select the Font menu.
2. Select the Bold, Underline, Double Underline, Italic, Redline, or Strikeout command from the menu. The enhancement is applied to the font shown on the Status line.
3. Begin typing the new text.
4. When you're ready to turn the feature off (that is, type more text without that enhancement), select the Normal command on the F**o**nt menu, or select the command for the feature again to turn it off.

Shortcuts When you want to use **B**old, **U**nderline, **I**talic, or **N**ormal, press the following speed keys, instead of using the F**o**nt menu, to turn the enhancement on and off.

Ctrl+N	Normal
Ctrl+B	Bold
Ctrl+I	Italic
Ctrl+U	Underline

Because the Outli**n**e, Shado**w**, and Small **C**ap enhancements are used less frequently, these enhancements are available only through the Font dialog box. (You can select more than one at once. See the section later in this lesson about using multiple enhancements.) Here's how to turn on these enhancements to apply to new text:

1. Select the Font command on the Font menu or press F9. WordPerfect for Windows displays the Font dialog box shown in Figure 10-1.
2. In the Appearance section of the dialog box, select the enhancement you want to use, then select OK.
3. Begin typing the new text.
4. When you're ready to turn the feature off, select the Normal command on the Font menu, or press Ctrl+N. The font shown on the Status line returns to normal.

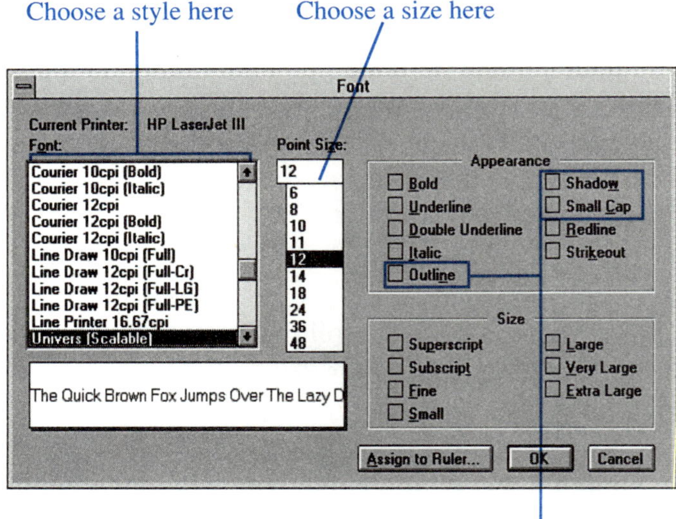

Figure 10-1 The Font dialog box.

Enhancing Existing Text

When you want to add an enhancement to text that you've already typed, you must select the text first, then enhance it. Use the same steps outlined in the preceding section, but select the text first. Here's how:

1. Select the text you want to enhance. The text is highlighted on your screen.

2. Open the Font menu.

3. If the enhacement you want appears as a command on the Font menu, select that command. If not, select the Font command to display the Font dialog box. Select an enhancement from the Appearance box, then select OK. WordPerfect for Windows returns to the document window and applies the enhancement to the selected text.

4. The text you chose in step 1 remains highlighted, so if you want to add another enhancement, repeat steps 2 and 3.

5. Move the cursor to a new location to unselect the selected text.

Don't Remember How to Select Text? Refer to Lesson 5.

Using Multiple Enhancements

There may be times when you want to turn on more than one enhancement at once. For example, suppose you want to type an entire paragraph in bold italic, and then underline it too. In a case like this, you can use the options in the Font dialog box to turn on more than one enhancement feature. Use the following steps.

1. Select the Font command on the Font menu or press F9. WordPerfect for Windows displays the Font dialog box.
2. In the Appearance box, select the enhancement features you want to use, then select OK.
3. Type the new text.
4. When you want to turn off the enhancement features you selected in step 1, select the Font command on the Font menu.
5. In the Appearance box, turn off the selected features by selecting them again. (These features toggle on and off each time you select them.) Select OK to return to your document.

Selecting Enhancements Quickly You can select bold, italic, and underline quickly by pressing Ctrl+B, Ctrl+I, or Ctrl+U.

You can apply multiple enhancements to existing text by selecting the text first, then following steps 1 and 2.

Lesson 11

Viewing WordPerfect for Windows Codes

In this lesson, you'll learn how to display hidden codes in a document and edit them when necessary.

What Are Codes?

When you add special formatting or other features, such as text enhancements to a document, WordPerfect for Windows keeps track of those features with *special codes*. For example, when you set a title in bold, WordPerfect for Windows inserts a `Bold On` code at the beginning of the title, and a `Bold Off` code at the end of the title.

Codes are not normally displayed on the screen, but there are times when it's necessary to view them. For instance, if you use a command that inserts a code in your document where another code already exists, the new code may be ignored. A good example of this is what might happen if you change a paragraph's margins from 1 1/2 inches to 2 inches. If the 2-inch code is inserted before the 1 1/2-inch code, WordPerfect for Windows reads the 1 1/2 inch code last. The 2-inch code, therefore, has no effect. When you view your document, you find that the paragraph hasn't been reformatted with 2-inch margins. By revealing the hidden codes, however, you can see immediately that you need to delete the old margin code. You might never find the solution to this problem without revealing the hidden codes.

If you're not sure what the codes revealed in your document mean, check the chart at the back of this book—it lists all hidden codes and their meanings.

Displaying and Hiding Codes

You can display hidden codes (and hide them again) in a document using the Reveal Codes command. Follow these steps:

1. Select the Reveal Codes command on the View menu. The document window is split horizontally. The hidden codes are shown in the lower half of the screen (see Figure 11-1).
2. To hide the codes and return to your document, select the Reveal Codes command from the View menu.

Revealing Codes Quickly In place of the Reveal Codes command on the View menu, press Alt+F3 to reveal hidden codes in a document. Press Alt+F3 again to turn off the Reveal Codes command.

When WordPerfect for Windows splits the document screen, the formatted document is displayed in the top half of the screen. The bottom half of the screen displays the unformatted text intermixed with the hidden codes in the document.

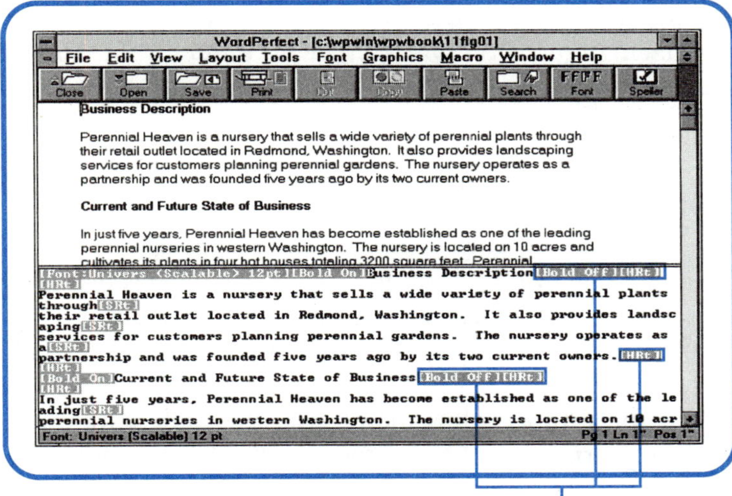

WordPerfect for Windows codes

Figure 11-1 The hidden codes are revealed in the bottom half of the window.

Working in the Reveal Codes Window

When using Reveal Codes, you can do any type of task in WordPerfect for Windows that you can do in the normal document window. You can edit, type, move text, enhance text, and use any of the menu commands. The text cursor appears in both sections of the screen. When you make a change, it is reflected in both sections of the screen.

WordPerfect for Windows uses several different types of hidden codes. For features that affect selected text, such as bold or italic, an *On* code, as well as an *Off* code, is used. Other codes simply mark the point where a *nonprinting character* appears, such as a tab or a hard return. As you continue to learn more WordPerfect for Windows techniques, you'll add more and more codes to your documents. In Figure 11-1, you can see the hidden codes for this document.

Editing Codes

The fact that you can edit the codes themselves can often save you time when you want to make changes in a document. For example, if you wanted to remove the bold enhancement from a phrase in a document, you would normally have to select the phrase, then select the menu command or speed key to remove the bold feature. But using Reveal Codes, you can remove the bold enhancement (or any other code) with a single keystroke. Here's how.

1. With the Reveal Codes window displayed on your screen, move the cursor to the code you want to remove.
2. Press Delete. The code is immediately removed.

Notice that when there is an on code as well as an off code, you don't have to delete both; just delete one and WordPerfect for Windows removes the other automatically.

Panic

Delete the Wrong Code? You can bring back a deleted code by using the Undo command you learned about in Lesson 6.

In this lesson, you learned what hidden codes are, and how to display and edit them. In the next lesson, you'll learn how to save, add to, and print selected blocks of text.

Lesson 12

Saving, Appending, and Printing Text Blocks

In this lesson, you'll learn how you can save, append, and print blocks of text, rather than an entire document.

Saving Blocks of Text

In Lesson 7, you learned how to save an entire document, but WordPerfect for Windows also enables you to save a portion of a document. This can be very useful, for example, when you want to save a paragraph or two from a large document under a different document name.

To save a portion of text, you'll use the Save Selected Text dialog box shown in Figure 12-1. The dialog box is almost identical to the Save As dialog box you used in Lesson 7. Here's how to save selected text:

1. With a document displayed in the document window, select the text you want to save under a new document name. The text is highlighted on the screen.
2. Select the Save or Save As command on the **F**ile menu. WordPerfect for Windows displays the Save Selected Text dialog box, shown in Figure 12-1.

3. Check to see that the current drive and directory is where you want to save the file. If not, select the correct drive and directory from the Directories list box.

4. In the Save As text box, type a name for the new document, then select Save. WordPerfect for Windows saves the selected text under the new document name.

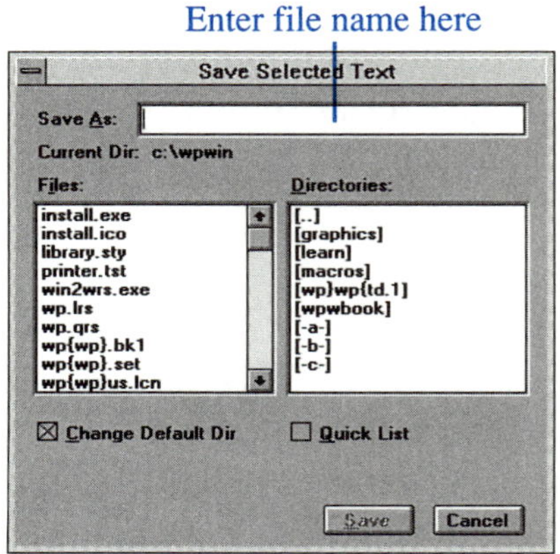

Figure 12-1 The Save Selected Text dialog box.

Appending Blocks of Text

In Lesson 6, you learned that when you use the Cut or the Copy command, WordPerfect for Windows places the selected text in the Windows Clipboard. You also learned that the selected text remains in the Clipboard only until you use the Cut or Copy command again, at which time the old Clipboard text is replaced with the new text you select. The Append command lets you add a copy of selected text to the end of the Clipboard.

Appending Text to the Clipboard The Append command allows you to add to existing text in the Clipboard without replacing text that's already there. You can use the command repeatedly to accumulate blocks of text in the Clipboard.

Here's an example of how and why you might want to use the Append command. Suppose you want to create a document that includes selected paragraphs from other documents. You can use the Append command to add the paragraphs you want into the Clipboard, and then use the Paste command to insert the entire collection into a new document.

Because *append* means to "add to," the Clipboard must contain at least one selection of text before you can use the Append command. The following steps describe how to place text into an empty Clipboard, and then use the Append command to add to it.

1. Open the document from which you want to select text.
2. Select the text you want to place in the Clipboard, then select the Copy command on the Edit menu, or select the Copy button on the Button Bar. The selected text is copied to the Clipboard.
3. Select the next text block you want to add to the Clipboard, then select the Append command on the Edit menu.
4. Repeat step 3 until all text is selected.
5. Paste the Clipboard contents where you want it, using the Paste command before using the Cut or Copy command again.

It might be helpful to display the Clipboard on the screen while you work through these steps. If you reduce the size of the WordPerfect for Windows screen, you can open the Clipboard window and place it on the screen along with the WordPerfect for Windows' screen. This allows you to see the selected text as it is appended to the Clipboard as shown in Figure 12-2. The Clipboard icon is located in the Main group, under the Windows Program Manager. If you need help opening the Clipboard, refer to your Windows documentation.

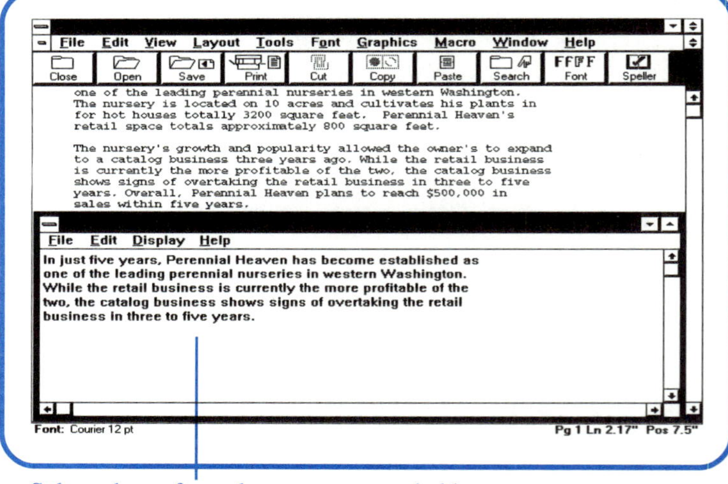

Figure 12-2 Text from the document is appended to the Clipboard.

Printing Blocks of Text

In WordPerfect for Windows, you can also print blocks of text rather than the whole document or selected pages. For example, if a page in a document contains a quotation, you can select the quotation and print it using the Print dialog box shown in Figure 12-3. Here's how.

1. With the document displayed in the document window, select the text you want to print. WordPerfect for Windows highlights the selected text on the screen.

2. Select the Print command on the **F**ile menu. The Print dialog box appears. In the Options area of the dialog box, notice that the Selected Text option is automatically chosen so you don't need to select it.

3. Select the Print button. WordPerfect for Windows prints the selected text.

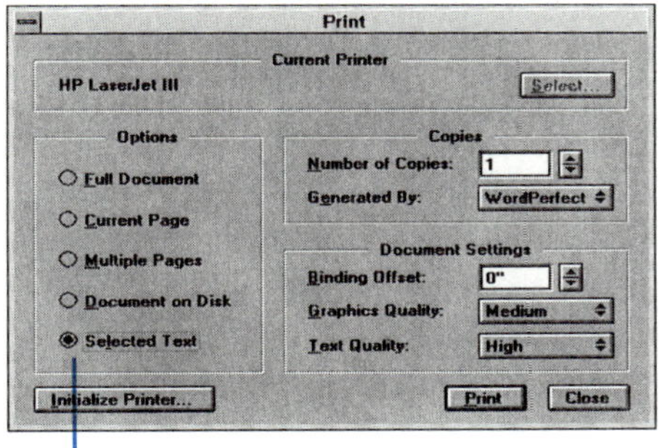

Figure 12-3 The Print dialog box.

This lesson has taught you how to save selected text, append selected text to the Clipboard, and print selected text. In Lesson 13, you'll learn the techniques that let you search for and replace text in a document.

Lesson 13

Searching for and Replacing Text

In this lesson, you'll learn how to find text in a document, and replace it with new text if you wish.

What is Search and Replace?

The Search and Replace feature in WordPerfect for Windows lets you search a document for any text—a character, word, phrase, and so on—and replace it with whatever text you choose. It's up to you whether you find and replace just one instance of the text, selected instances, or all instances. If you don't want to replace the text, you can use the Search feature by itself to find the text.

Searching for Text

As mentioned earlier, you can use the Search feature without replacing text. Let's see how that feature works before moving on to searching and replacing.

When you use the Search feature, the Search dialog box, shown in Figure 13-1, appears.

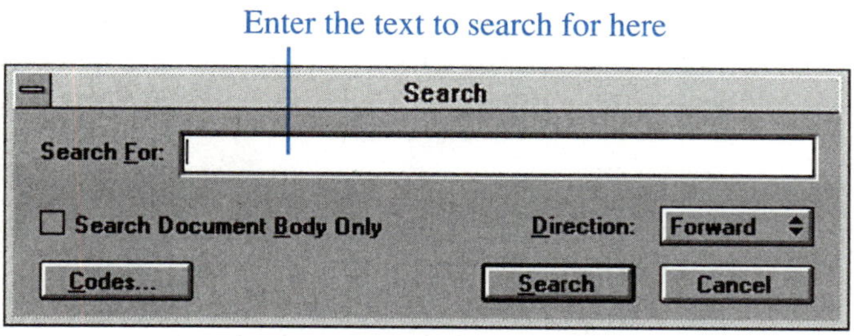

Enter the text to search for here

Search

Search For:

Search Document Body Only

Direction: Forward

Codes...

Search

Cancel

Figure 13-1 The Search dialog box.

In the Search dialog box, you enter the text to search for and you can change the search direction from forward to backward. WordPerfect for Windows is set up to search forward from the point of the cursor. If you want to search the entire document, reposition the cursor at the beginning of the document by pressing Ctrl+Home, then start the search. If the cursor is near the end of the document and you want to find text on a previous page, leave the cursor at its current position and search backwards. Here's how to begin a search:

1. Move the cursor to the location where you want to begin the search.
2. Select the Search command on the **E**dit menu to display the Search dialog box.
3. Type the text you want to find in the Search For text box.
4. If you want to search backwards, select **B**ackward **D**irection.

5. Select the Search button to begin the search. WordPerfect for Windows finds the first instance of the text and moves the cursor there.

Search Shortcut To display the Search dialog box with one keystroke, press F2.

What WordPerfect for Windows Finds

If the text you search for (that is, the text you enter in the Search For text box in the Search dialog box) contains uppercase characters, such as in the word *Business,* WordPerfect for Windows searches only for an instance that matches exactly. If the document also contains the word *business,* that text is not found. When the text you search for contains no uppercase characters, WordPerfect for Windows searches for any instance, whether uppercase or not. So, for example, if you search for *business,* WordPerfect searches for *business* and *Business.*

Continuing a Search

When you use the **S**earch command, WordPerfect for Windows finds only the first instance of the text. But what if you want to continue searching the document for additional instances? You can continue the search by:

1. Continue searching for the next instance by selecting the Search Next command on the **E**dit menu. WordPerfect for Windows finds the next instance.
2. To return to the previous instance, select the Search Previous command on the **E**dit menu.

3. Continue selecting Search Next or Search Previous until the instances you're looking for are found.

Search Shortcuts Press Shift+F2 in place of the Search Next command, and Alt+F2 in place of the Search Previous command.

Searching for Codes

You may find it helpful to search for a WordPerfect for Windows hidden code rather than for text. Use these steps to search for a code in a document.

1. Press Ctrl+Home to move the cursor to the beginning of the document.
2. Select the Search command on the Edit menu, or select the Search button on the Button Bar, to display the Search dialog box.
3. When the Search dialog box appears, select the Codes button to display the Codes dialog box.
4. Select a code, then select Insert. WordPerfect for Windows inserts the code in the Search For text box.
5. Select Close in the Codes dialog box to return to the Search dialog box.
6. Select the Search button. WordPerfect for Windows moves the cursor to the point where the code was inserted in the document.

You must use the Codes dialog box to insert the code in the Search For text box. If you type, for example, [Bold On] in the Search For text box, WordPerfect for Windows thinks you're looking for the text phrase *Bold On* enclosed in brackets, rather than the code itself.

It isn't necessary to select Reveal Codes to use the steps just described. You can search for codes whether the Reveal Codes feature is on or off.

Replacing Text

In many cases, it's very useful to have WordPerfect for Windows search for and replace text for you. For example, suppose you want to create two versions of a document and change only the company name. You can create the first document, save it under a different name from the second document, then search for and replace the company name in the second document. Selecting the Replace command displays the Search and Replace dialog box, shown in Figure 13-2.

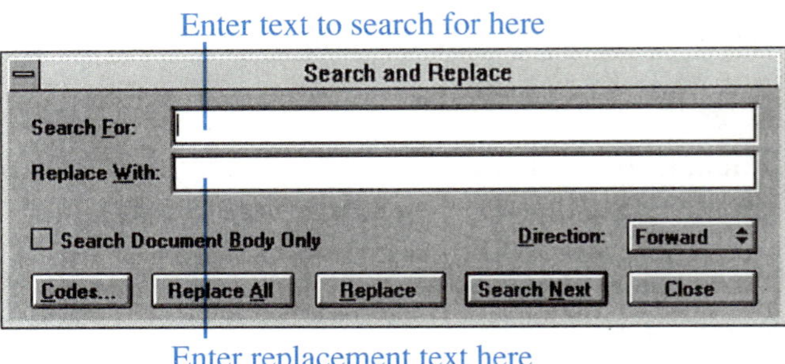

Figure 13-2 The Search and Replace dialog box.

Use the following steps to search and replace.

1. With the document displayed in the active window, press Ctrl+Home to move the cursor to the beginning of the document.

2. Select the Replace command on the Edit menu or press Ctrl+F2 to display the Search and Replace dialog box.

3. Type the text to search for in the Search For dialog box.

4. Type the replacement text in the Replace With dialog box.

5. Select Search Next. WordPerfect for Windows stops and highlights at the first instance of the text you're searching for. The Search and Replace dialog box remains on the screen.

6. Select Replace. WordPerfect for Windows replaces the first instance with the replacement text, and automatically moves to the next instance.

7. Select Replace again. WordPerfect for Windows replaces the instance again, and moves on to the next instance.

8. To cancel Replace at any time, select Close.

You can search for and replace hidden codes using these steps if you use the Codes button in place of steps 4 and 5.

Lesson 14

Setting Up the Page Layout of a Document

In this lesson, you'll learn when and how to select the paper size for a document, and how to set the top, bottom, right, and left margins.

Understanding Page Layout

The *page layout* of a document refers to the settings that affect how the document looks on the printed page. The two settings that affect page layout are the *paper size* and the *margins*.

When to Set Page Layout It's best to set paper size and margins before you create a document so you can see how the document will be laid out. If you change these settings after the document is created, the text is reformatted to fit the new margin and paper size settings, but some document characteristics (such as tabs and page breaks) may not reformat correctly.

Selecting a Paper Size

Because most documents are printed on 8 1/2-by-11-inch paper, WordPerfect for Windows uses this paper size as its default. If you use this paper size (sometimes called *standard*), you don't need to change the setting for paper size.

However, if you want to print on, for example, 8 1/2-by-14-inch paper, commonly used for legal documents, you need to select the correct paper size. You also must set the paper size for custom or nonstandard paper sizes. In addition, if you want to print sideways on any type of paper, the paper size must be changed. When you change the paper size, it affects only the current document. Here's how:

1. Choose the Page command on the Layout menu. When the submenu appears, select the Paper Size command. WordPerfect for Windows displays the Paper Size dialog box, shown in Figure 14-1.

2. Select the correct paper size, then the Select button. WordPerfect for Windows readjusts the paper size for the current document.

Print Sideways? Note that not all printers are capable of printing sideways. Check your printer manual to be sure.

In the dialog box, WordPerfect for Windows distinguishes sideways (*landscape*) paper sizes by printing the sample letter A on its side. Notice also, that the page dimensions are reversed. When you print sideways on standard paper, the dimensions are 11-by 8-1/2 instead of 8 1/2-by-11.

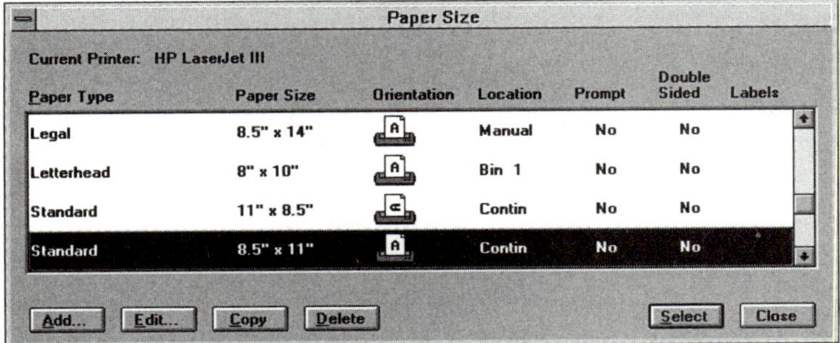

Figure 14-1 The Paper Size dialog box.

Creating a Custom Paper Size

If you frequently use a nonstandard paper size, such as custom letterhead or stationery, you can create a custom paper size using the Paper Size dialog box. To do this, follow these steps.

1. Select the Page command on the **L**ayout menu. When the submenu appears, select the Paper Size command. WordPerfect for Windows displays the Paper Size dialog box.

2. Select the Add button. WordPerfect for Windows displays the Add Paper Size dialog box, shown in Figure 14-2.

3. In the dialog box, choose a name in the Paper **T**ype box.

4. Choose a setting in the Paper Orientation box.

5. Specify the correct paper dimensions in the Paper Size box.

6. If necessary, enter the correct settings for Paper Location, Text Adjustments, and Print Options, then select OK. WordPerfect for Windows returns to the Paper Size dialog box, and displays the entry you just added to the list.

7. Select Close to return to the document window.

The entry you added is now available in the Page Size dialog box each time you want to print/create a WordPerfect for Windows document.

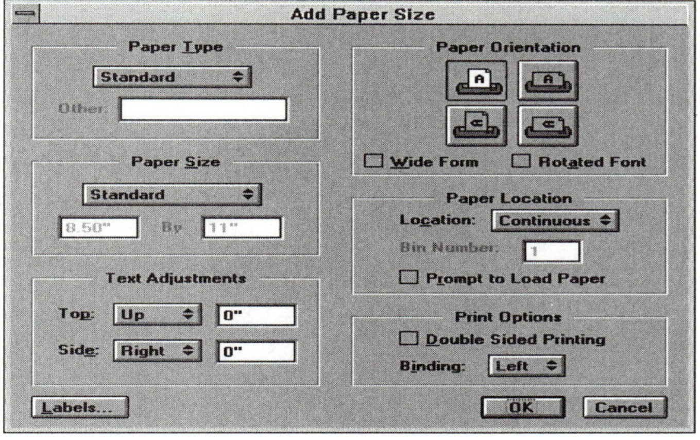

Figure 14-2 The Add Paper Size dialog box.

Setting Margins

Margins are the areas of white space that border the text on the page. By default, WordPerfect for Windows sets each margin to one inch when you create a new document. In most cases, you shouldn't need to alter the margin widths, but there are times when it might be necessary.

For example, you might want to change a margin in order to align text with a logo or other graphical enhancement on letterhead paper. You can change the top, bottom, right, and left margins independently by following these steps:

1. Select the **M**argins command on the **L**ayout menu. WordPerfect for Windows displays the Margins dialog box, shown in Figure 14-3.

2. In the dialog box, enter a number for the margins you want to change. When all settings are correct, select OK. WordPerfect for Windows automatically adjusts the margins for the current document.

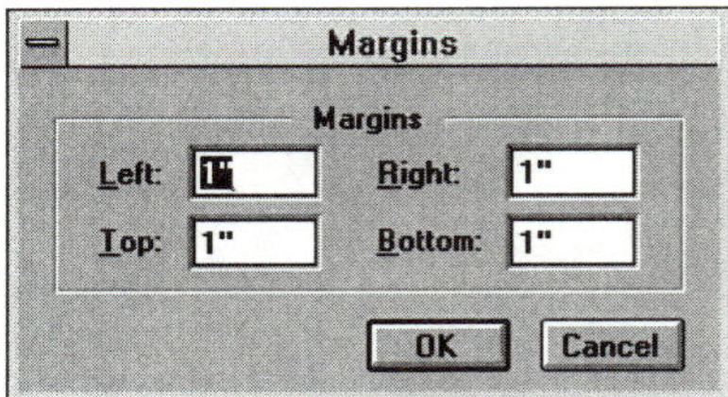

Figure 14-3 The Margins dialog box.

Lesson 15

Setting Tabs

In this lesson, you'll learn what the ruler is and how to use it to set tabs in a document.

What Are Tabs?

A *tab* is a point on a line to which the cursor moves when you press Tab. Tabs are used for aligning special text, such as in a simple list, or a table like Table 15-1. Tabs come in four different types, described in Table 15-1.

Table 15-1 Tab Types and Their Function.

Tab Type	Result
Left-aligned	Text aligns at the tab and moves to the right as you enter new text
Right-aligned	Text aligns at the tab and moves to the left as you enter new text
Center	Text aligns at the tab and centers itself around the tab as you enter new text
Decimal	When entering numbers, they align at the tab and move to the left until you insert a decimal point (period); subsequent numbers move to the right

Table 15-2 illustrates sample text using the four types of tabs described in Table 15-1.

Table 15-2 Text Aligned at the Four Tab Positions.

Left Tab	Right Tab	Center Tab	Decimal Tab
This text is typed at a left- aligned tab	This text is typed at a right- aligned tab	This text is typed at a center tab	8.3 2987 .009 98.23

In WordPerfect for Windows, left-aligned tabs are automatically set every half inch when you create a new document. You can clear these tabs, move them, or set your own, as you'll learn later in this lesson. First, let's look at the *ruler* in WordPerfect for Windows.

Displaying the Ruler

When you start WordPerfect for Windows, the ruler isn't automatically displayed on the screen. When the ruler is displayed, it appears just above the text area in the document window.

What is the Ruler? The ruler is a gauge that measures a page horizontally. It displays all tab settings, as well as right and left margin settings. You use the ruler to modify any of these settings.

Follow these steps to display the ruler:

- Select the Ruler command on the View menu.

  Or,

- Press Alt+Shift+F3.

Figure 15-1 illustrates the ruler in a document window, and identifies each of the settings and the tab buttons.

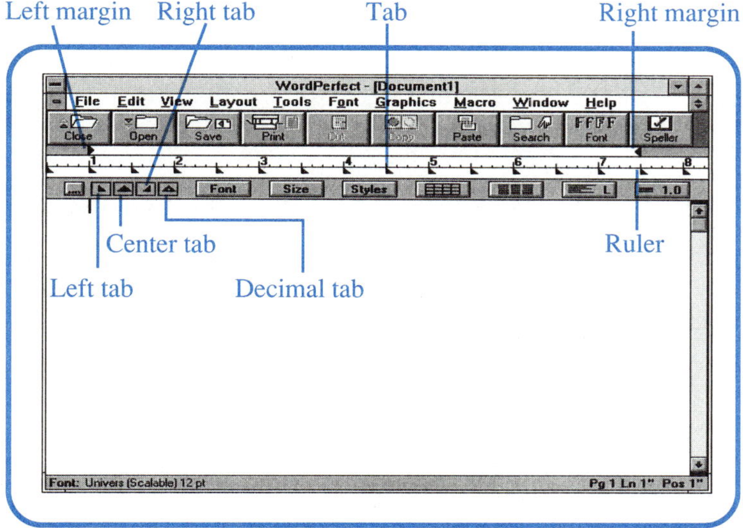

Figure 15-1 The ruler in the document window.

Clearing Tabs

When you enter certain types of text, the WordPerfect for Windows ruler can seem rather cluttered with tabs at every half inch. For example, to enter a two-column table like the one shown in Table 15-1, you need only two tabs. It's often helpful to clear some of the preset tabs out of the way before entering text. Here's how:

1. Display the ruler in the document window by selecting the Ruler command on the **V**iew menu.

2. Point to the tab you want to clear and drag it off the ruler towards the text area. When you release the mouse button, the tab is cleared.

Moving, Adding, and Deleting Tabs Once you have formatted text using tabs, be very careful when moving, adding, and deleting them. If, for example, your document contains a table with four columns of text and you delete one of the tabs, the table will not reformat correctly.

If you are resetting the entire ruler with new tabs, you can quickly clear off all tabs at once using these steps.

1. Display the ruler in the document window by selecting the Ruler command on the **V**iew menu.

2. Double-click on any tab on the ruler. WordPerfect for Windows displays the Tab Set dialog box, shown in Figure 15-2. (You can also display this dialog box by selecting the Line command on the **L**ayout menu, then the Tab Set command.)

3. In the dialog box, select the Clear Tabs button, then select OK. WordPerfect for Windows clears all tabs from the ruler in the document window.

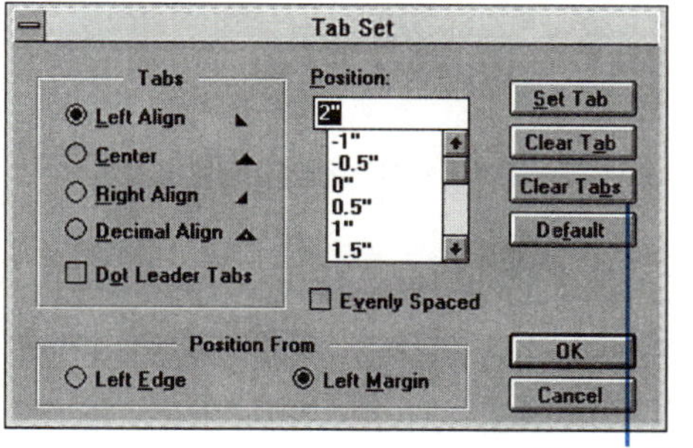

Figure 15-2 The Tab Set dialog box.

Setting Tabs

When you want to use tabs other than those preset at every half inch, you need to set new tabs. The tabs you set affect the current paragraph and remain in effect until you either change them, or encounter subsequent text for which different tabs have been set. To set new tabs in a document:

1. With the document ruler displayed on the screen, place the cursor at the location where the new tabs will be set.

2. Follow the steps described earlier to clear all tabs.

3. When all tabs are cleared from the ruler, point to and drag a Tab button from the Button Bar into the ruler.

4. Position the tab where you want it to appear on the ruler, then release the mouse button.

5. Repeat steps 3 and 4 to set more tabs.

In the sample business plan document shown in Figure 15-3, preset tabs were cleared and left-aligned tabs were set at 1 1/2 and 3 inches to format the new text.

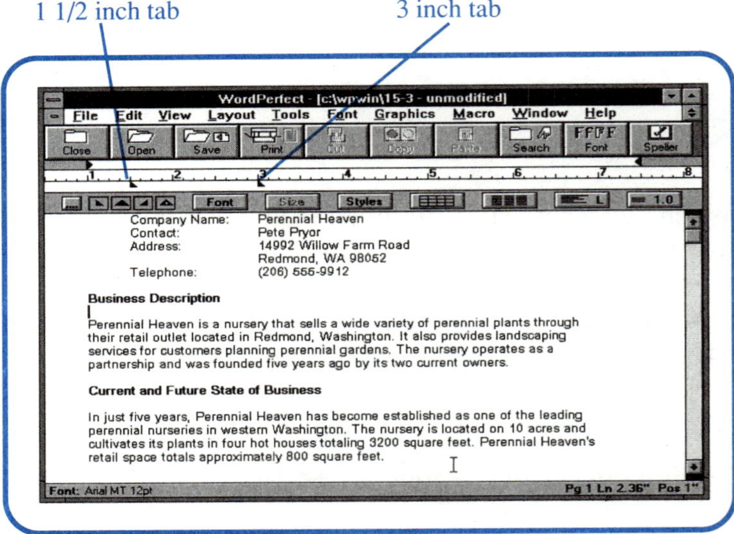

Figure 15-3 The sample business plan document displaying tabular text.

If you prefer to set tabs using the menu command:

1. Select the Line command on the **L**ayout menu, then select the Tab Set command from the submenu. WordPerfect displays the Tab Set dialog box. The **P**osition box displays all current tab settings.

2. Select Clear Tabs to delete all tabs.

3. In the Tabs box, select the type of tab you want to set.

4. Enter a positon number (in inches) in the **P**osition text box, then select Set Tab.

5. Repeat steps 3 and 4 to set more tabs, then select OK to return to the document window.

Moving Tabs

Often it's not necessary to clear all tabs and reset new ones; you can simply move existing tabs. Here's how:

1. With the ruler displayed in the document window, click on the tab you want to move and drag it to a new location (either right or left on the ruler). As you move the tab along the ruler, notice a vertical line appears in the document window to help you position the tab.

2. When the tab is correctly positioned, release the mouse button. The tab moves to its new position.

Adding Dot Leaders

A *dot leader* is used when you want the space between tabs filled in with dots. Dot leaders are usually used when entering values, as illustrated in the example below:

Item .... Quantity

Shasta Daisy 14

Veronica 12

Astilbe 15

Campanula 8

To set tabs with dot leaders, follow these steps:

1. Display the ruler in the document window by selecting the **R**uler command on the **V**iew menu.
2. Place the cursor in the document where you want the new tab set.
3. Click on the Dot leader button on the ruler Button Bar. Notice dots are added to each of the tab buttons in the Button Bar.
4. Click and drag a Tab button into the ruler, releasing it where you want the tab to be set. When you return to the document and press Tab for the tab just set, it will be preceded by dots. Note that other tabs on the ruler remain unchanged.

Specifying Dot Leaders If you use the Tab Set dialog box to set tabs, you can specify dot leaders by selecting the **D**ot Leader Tabs check box.

The Dot leader button toggles on and off each time you select it, so to remove the dot leaders from the Tab buttons, select the Dot leader button again.

Lesson 16

Aligning Text

This lesson teaches you how to indent and justify text in various ways, and set line spacing in a document.

Indenting Text

In WordPerfect for Windows, text can be indented in a number of ways:

- Indent the first line of a paragraph from the left margin.
- Indent the entire paragraph from the left margin.
- Indent the entire paragraph from both the left and right margins.
- Indent all lines except the first line in a paragraph—commonly called a *hanging indent.*

Indenting the first line of a paragraph is easy; just press Tab. WordPerfect for Windows moves the cursor to the first tab position where you can start entering text. When you reach the end of the first line, the text wraps to the left margin on the next line. No special command is needed for a first-line indent. For the other types of indents, WordPerfect for Windows provides options under the Paragraph command on the **L**ayout menu, as shown in Figure 16-1.

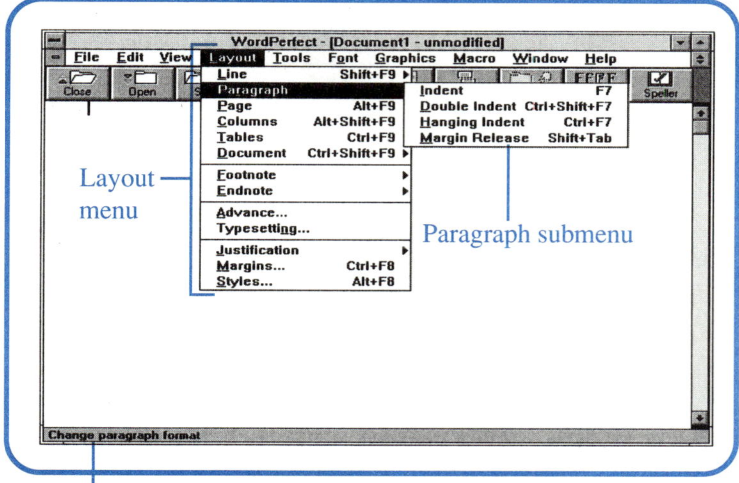

Figure 16-1 The Paragraph submenu.

Using these commands—**I**ndent, **D**ouble indent, and **H**anging indent—you can indent text in one of two ways: before you type the text or after the text has been typed. These are the steps for setting an indent style *before* the text is typed.

1. Place the cursor at the position in the document where you want to indent text.

2. Select the Paragraph command on the **L**ayout menu.

3. When the submenu is displayed, select an indent style.

4. Begin typing. The paragraph conforms to the indent style you chose. When you press Enter to end the paragraph, the cursor returns to the left margin.

To apply an indent style to existing text, follow these steps:

1. Place the cursor at the beginning of the first line of the paragraph.

2. Select the Paragraph command on the **L**ayout menu.

3. When the submenu is displayed, select an indent style. WordPerfect for Windows reformats the paragraph to the indent style you choose.

Setting Indents Quickly Use the following speed keys to select an indent style quickly.

Indent	**F7**
Double Indent	**Ctrl+Shift+F7**
Hanging Indent	**Ctrl+F7**

Changing an Indent Style

When you apply an indent style to a paragraph, WordPerfect for Windows inserts a hidden indent code at the beginning of the paragraph. You can change an indent style at any time by deleting the hidden code and replacing it, if you like, with a new one. Follow these steps to change an indent style.

1. Position the cursor at the beginning of the first line of the paragraph. (Press Home on the first line of the paragraph.)

2. Press **Delete** to delete the code for the indent style you applied to the paragraph. WordPerfect for Windows realigns the text to its normal unindented style.

3. If you want to apply a new indent style, select a style using the **Paragraph** command on the **Layout** menu. The text is realigned to the style you chose.

Correct Codes When you change an indent style, it's a good idea to use the Reveal Codes command, so that you can see the existing indent codes you are deleting. It's best to clear out old codes before applying new ones to be sure your paragraph reformats correctly.

Choosing a Justification Style

Justification refers to the way text lines up at the left and right edges of a paragraph. WordPerfect for Windows offers four justification styles:

Style	Result
Left	Lines up text on the left margin, but leaves the right margin ragged.
Right	Aligns text at the right margin, but leaves a ragged left margin.
Center	Centers text between the left and right margins.
Full	Aligns text on both the left and right margins by adding spaces between words where necessary.

WordPerfect for Windows automatically uses left justification for all new text you enter in a document. You can change a paragraph's justification by applying any of the styles just described. Each one is illustrated graphically in Figure 16-2.

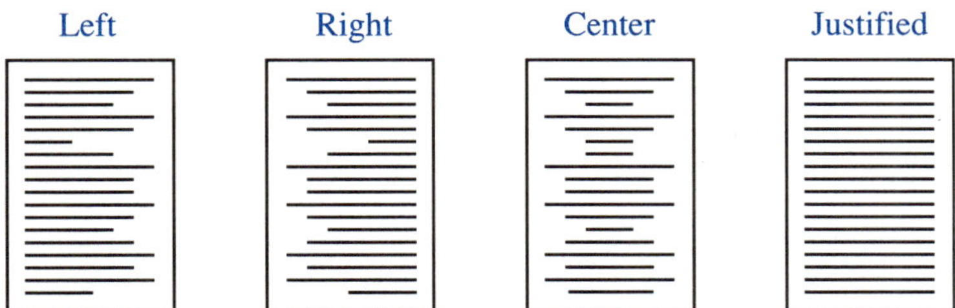

Figure 16-2 Left-aligned, right-aligned, centered, and justified text.

The quickest way to change justification is by using the Justification button on the ruler (see Figure 16-3). Here's how:

1. With the document displayed in the document window, move the cursor to the beginning of the paragraph to justify.

2. Display the ruler by selecting the **R**uler command on the **V**iew menu.

3. Select the Justification button (marked L for left) and choose a justification style from the drop-down menu. WordPerfect for Windows immediately rejustifies the paragraph.

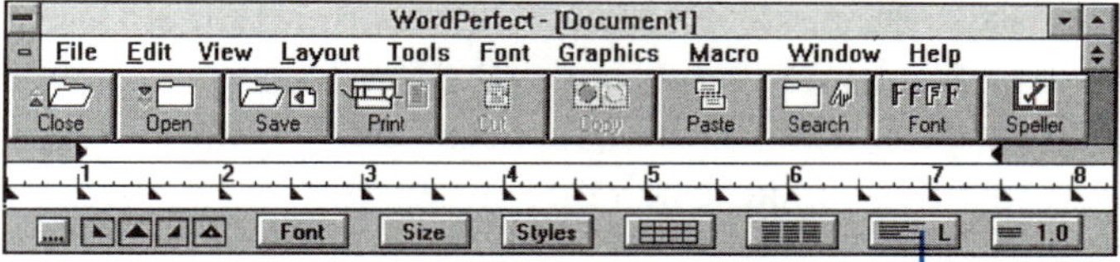

Figure 16-3 Justification button.

You can also set justification using menu commands by following these steps:

1. With the document displayed in the document window, move the cursor to the beginning of the paragraph to justify.
2. Select the Justification command on the **L**ayout menu.
3. When the submenu appears, select a justification style. WordPerfect for Windows rejustifies the paragraph.

Shortcuts In place of steps 2 and 3, you can use one of the following speed keys to select a justification style:

Ctrl+R Right
Ctrl+J Center
Ctrl+F Full
Ctrl+L Left

Setting Document Line Spacing

Most documents, such as letters and memos, are single-spaced, meaning there are no blank lines between the lines of text. This is the standard line spacing WordPerfect for Windows uses for all new documents. However, sometimes it's helpful to double-space or triple-space a document, adding blank lines between the lines of text. This is common in draft documents so that handwritten comments can be entered. There are two ways to change the line spacing in a document: using the Spacing button on the ruler or using a menu command. Let's look at the ruler method first, using a new document.

1. Open a new WordPerfect for Windows document.
2. Display the ruler by selecting the **R**uler command on the **V**iew menu.
3. Before typing any text, choose a line spacing option (1, 1.5, or 2) by selecting the Spacing button on the ruler. The spacing you choose appears in the Line spacing button on the ruler.
4. Begin typing text. The text you type conforms to the line spacing you chose.

Using the **S**pacing menu command rather than the button on the ruler, you have more line spacing choices than just 1, 1.5, and 2. In fact, your choices are practically unlimited.

1. Open a new WordPerfect for Windows document.
2. Select the Line command on the **L**ayout menu.
3. When the submenu appears, select the Spacing command. The Line Spacing dialog box appears.
4. To set the spacing, enter a number in the Spacing box, or click on the up or down arrow to select a number, then select OK. (The arrows move in 0.5 increments.) If your ruler is displayed, the spacing you choose appears in the **S**pacing button on the ruler.

5. Begin typing text. The text appears in the chosen line spacing.

Setting Line Spacing for Selected Text

You have just learned how to set line spacing for an entire document, but you can also set line spacing for portions of a document, such as a paragraph. Here's how to set line spacing for a new paragraph.

1. Move the cursor to the point where you want to type the paragraph.
2. Use either the Spacing button on the ruler or the menu command to set the line spacing. If the ruler is displayed, the spacing you choose appears in the Line spacing button.
3. Enter text for the paragraph.
4. Reset the line spacing to the previous setting, if desired.

It's even easier to set line spacing when the paragraph has already been typed. Follow these steps.

1. Move the cursor anywhere within the paragraph.
2. Select the line spacing using either the Spacing button on the ruler or the menu command. If the ruler is displayed, the spacing you choose appears in the Line spacing button. The spacing affects only the current paragraph. (Notice how the number displayed in the Line spacing button on the ruler changes when you move the cursor to a new location.)

Lesson 17

Working with Fonts

In this lesson, you'll learn what a font is and how to choose a font for an entire document or for selected blocks of text.

Understanding Fonts

You can enhance the appearance and improve the readability of a document by using different *fonts* for the text. WordPerfect for Windows lets you change the font for a selected area of text, or for an entire document.

Fonts A font is the set of all characters that share a specific typeface, size, slant, and weight. The *typeface* refers to the design or style, the size is measured in *points* (one point equals 1/72 inch), the *slant* is either upright or italic, and the *weight* can range from light to extra bold. For example, Helvetica is a typeface, 14 is a point size, italic is a slant, and bold is a weight. Together, these characteristics—Helvetica 14 italic bold—are referred to as a font.

All printers are capable of printing at least one font. Most printers are capable of printing more than one font, even if it's just bold. To find out which fonts your printer can print, check your printer manual.

Selecting a Font for a Document

The first time you create a WordPerfect for Windows document, the text you type is displayed in the Courier 10 font, shown in Figure 17-1.

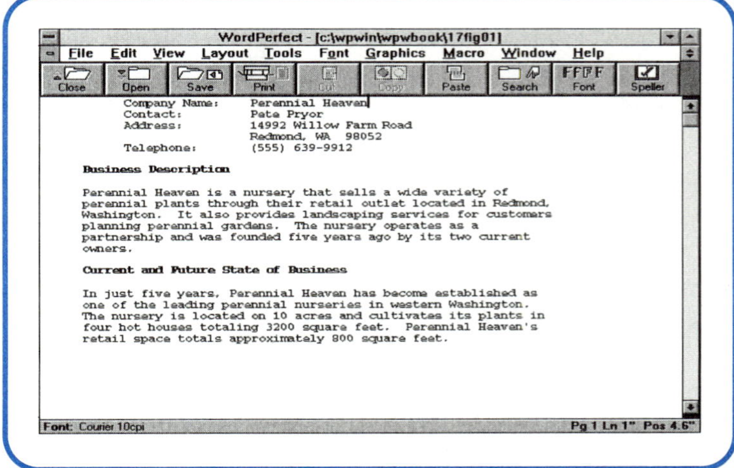

Figure 17-1 Text shown in the Courier 10 font.

You can change the font for an entire document—whether it's new or one you've already saved—by using the following steps.

1. Open a new document or recall an existing WordPerfect for Windows document.
2. Select the Document command on the **L**ayout menu, then choose Initial **F**ont. The Document Initial Font dialog box appears.
3. The fonts shown in the Fonts list box are those available on your printer.

4. Select a font. The sample text below the Fonts list box illustrates the selected font.

5. If the font you choose is scalable, select a size in the Point Size box, then select OK to return to your document. The font you chose in step 4 is displayed on the Status line.

Scalable Fonts In WordPerfect, a "scalable" font is one that's available in a variety of point sizes in the Font dialog box. You can choose a size from the Point Size list, or you can enter a size in the box at the top of the list.

If the document contains existing text, that text is now displayed in the new font. If the document is new, the new text you type will be displayed in the new font.

Unchanged text? If you find in an existing document that the font for some of the text didn't change, the document must contain a font code *preceding* that text. Use Reveal Codes to find and delete any hidden font codes. Once the code is removed, the font will be corrected.

Selecting a Default Font

If you prefer to use a font other than WordPerfect for Windows' default font, you can change the default font. When you change the default font, all new documents you create use the font you chose. (The current document, if any, is not changed when you use these steps.) Here's how.

1. Choose the Select Printer command on the **F**ile menu. The Select Printer dialog box appears.

2. Select the Setup button. The Printer Setup dialog box appears.

3. Select the Initial Font button. The Printer Initial Font dialog box appears.

4. Select a font from the Fonts list box. The sample text below the Fonts list box illustrates the selected font.

5. If the font you choose is scalable, select a size in the Point Size box, then select OK to close the dialog box. WordPerfect for Windows returns you to the Printer Setup dialog box.

6. The font you chose in step 4 is now displayed in the Current Initial Font box. Select OK to close this dialog box. WordPerfect for Windows returns you to the Select Printer dialog box.

7. Select Close to return to the document window.

Changing a Font for Selected Text

Different fonts are often used within a document to enhance text, or call attention to words or phrases in a document. For example, in this book, new terms appear in *italic*. If your document contains a quotation, a note, or a caution, you might want to call attention to it by displaying it in a different font. Here's how to apply a different font to selected text using the Font dialog box.

1. With the document displayed in the document window, select the text you want to change.

2. Select the Font command on the Font menu, or press F9. The Font dialog box, shown in Figure 17-2, appears.

3. Select a font from the Font list box. The sample text below the Font list box illustrates the selected font.

4. If the font you choose is scalable, select a size from the Point Size box, then select OK to return to your document. The paragraph you selected is now displayed in the new font.

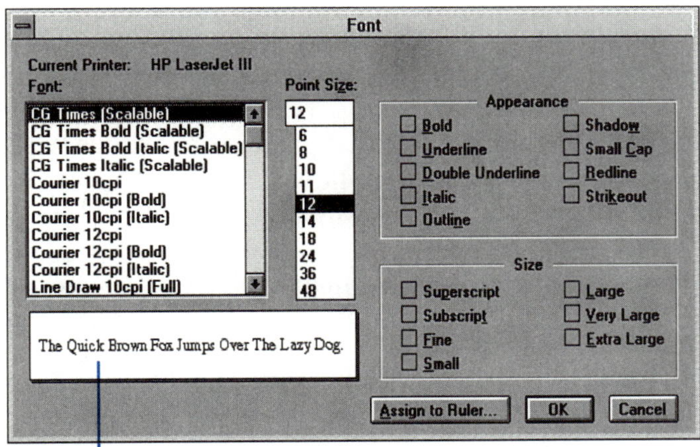

Figure 17-2 The Font dialog box.

These steps were used to change headings in the sample business plan document to Universe 14 Bold. The business plan now looks like the one shown in Figure 17-3.

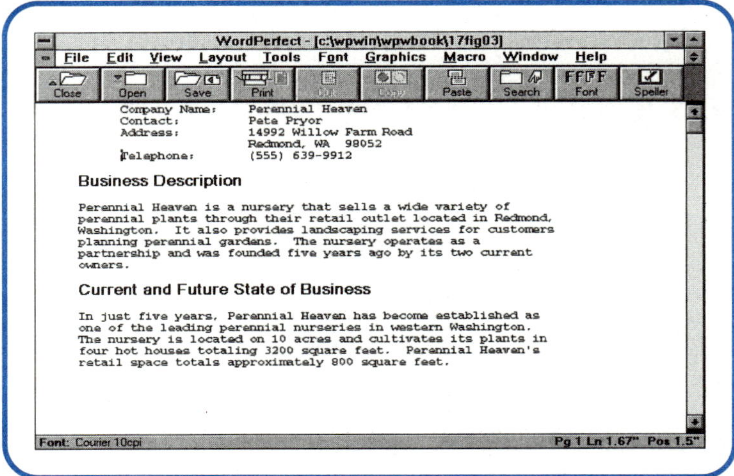

Figure 17-3 Headings are shown in the Universe 14 bold font.

You can also use the Font dialog box to change the font for new text you type. Just follow steps 2, 3, and 4 to open the dialog box and choose a font, then type the new text. When you're finished entering new text, be sure to recall the Font dialog box and change the font back to it's previous setting.

Adding Enhancements to a Font

Figure 17-2 illustrates settings for Appearance and Size in the Font dialog box. Whenever you use the preceding steps to select a new font, you can also assign a special size or appearance to the font, by selecting one of these options before you close the dialog box.

To see the affect of each of the Appearance and Size options, open the Font dialog box and select each one of the options. To turn off an option, select it again. The sample text illustrates the enhancement applied to the selected font.

Adding Fonts to the Ruler

When you learned about the ruler in Lesson 14, you might have noticed that the ruler contains a Font button. If you typically display the ruler in a document, you might find the Font button quicker to use for selecting a font. Before you can use the Font button, you must add fonts to the ruler using these steps:

1. Display the ruler in the document window, by selecting the Ruler command on the View menu.
2. Select the Font command on the Font menu, or press F9. The Fonts dialog box appears.
3. Select the Assign to Ruler button. The Ruler Fonts Menu dialog box appears. The Font List box lists all available fonts. The Fonts on Ruler box lists all fonts currently assigned to the ruler.
4. From the Font List box, select a font to add to the ruler, then select the Add button. The font is added to the Fonts on Ruler list.
5. Repeat steps 3 and 4 to add additional fonts to the ruler, then select OK. WordPerfect for Windows returns you to the Font dialog box.

6. Select OK to return to the document window. Now you can select the Font button on the ruler to choose a new font.

The Font button only lists fonts. If the font you choose is scalable, you must also use the Size button to change the font size. Follow these steps to use the ruler buttons.

1. Display the ruler in the document window.
2. Move the cursor to the point where you want new text to appear in the new font, or select existing text to change.
3. Select the Font button, then select a font from the list. WordPerfect for Windows changes the font of existing text, if any. The Status line indicates the new font name.
4. If the font you choose is scalable, select the Size button, then select a size from the list.

Lesson 18

Adding Headers and Footers to a Document

In this lesson, you'll learn how to add headers and footers to a document.

What Are Headers and Footers?

A *header* is repetitive information that appears on the first line of every page in a document. A *footer* is also repetitive information, but appears on the last, instead of the first, line of each page. Headers and footers might contain a title, a page number, a date, or a message of some kind, such as "Company Confidential."

When you create a header or footer, it automatically appears on every page of the document unless you specify otherwise. You can specify that your header or footer appears only on odd numbered pages or only on even numbered pages, as you'll learn in a later section of this lesson.

You can enhance header and footer text or apply special characteristics, just like you can to any text in the body of the document. So, for example, header and footer text can be centered, underlined, made bold, or right-aligned. In the examples that follow, you'll add some of these special features.

Creating Simple Headers and Footers

Use the following steps to create a simple header.

1. Select the Page command on the **L**ayout menu.
2. When the submenu appears, select the Headers dialog box as shown in Figure 18-1. The Headers dialog box appears.
3. Select Create to create Header A. (Notice in Figure 18.1 Header A is already selected in the dialog box.) A new window appears for Header A and the Title bar reads `Header A`.
4. Type the text for the header. You can select the text and add any enhancement or formatting such as bold or right-align.
5. Select Close to return to the document window.

To create a footer, follow the same steps just outlined, but select the **F**ooters, rather than the **H**eader command, in step 2.

Header and footer text can be one line or multiple lines. You can do anything to the text that you can do in the document window. That is, you can apply alignment styles, add enhancement features, and change the font of the text.

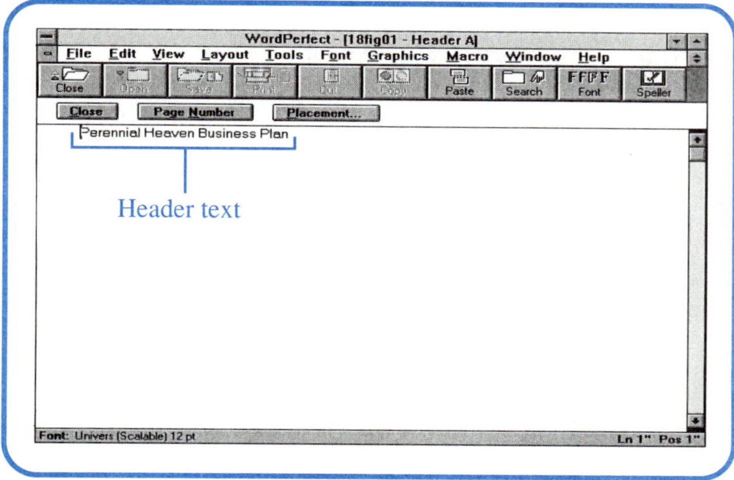

Figure 18-1 A Header window.

Inserting Page Numbers in Headers and Footers

Quite often a header or footer includes a page number. To insert a page number, use these steps.

1. Follow the steps given in the previous section for creating a header or footer.

2. When the header or footer window is displayed, position the cursor where you want the page number to appear, then select the Page Number button. WordPerfect for Windows inserts the code `^B`, as illustrated in Figure 18-2.

3. Select the Close button to return to the document window. WordPerfect for Windows places the correct page number on each page when the document is printed.

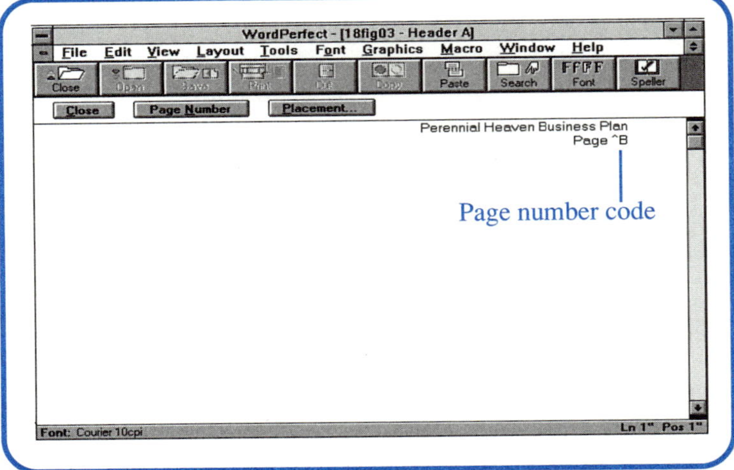

Figure 18-2 A page number code is included in this header.

Note that page numbers can also be inserted in a document without using headers and footers. You'll learn how to do this in Lesson 19.

Creating Two Headers or Footers

In some cases, you might want a different header or footer on facing pages of a document. For example, you might want to print a document title on odd numbered pages, and the chapter number on even numbered pages. In such cases, you create two separate headers or footers: header A and B, or footer A and B. Here's how to create two different footers in a document. (To use these steps to create a header, choose the Headers command from the Layout menu.)

1. Select the Page command on the Layout menu.
2. When the submenu appears, select the Footers command. The Footers dialog box appears.
3. Select Create to create Footer A. (Notice Footer A is already selected in the dialog box.) A new window for Footer A appears. The Title bar reads `Footer A`.
4. Type the text for the footer.
5. Select the Placement button. The Placement dialog box appears.
6. In the dialog box, select the Odd Pages option, then select OK.
7. Select the Close button in the Footer A window. WordPerfect for Windows returns you to the document window.
8. Select the Page command on the Layout menu.
9. Select Footers.
10. Select Footer B, then choose Create. A new window for Footer B appears. The Title bar reads `Footer B`.
11. At the left margin, enter the footer text.
12. Select the Placement button. The Placement dialog box appears.

13. In the Placement dialog box, select Even Pages, then select OK.

14. In the Footer B window, select Close. WordPerfect for Windows returns you to the document window.

When printing this document, Footer A appears on odd numbered pages, and Footer B on even numbered pages.

Header/Footer Pileup To avoid multiple headers or footers printing on top of each other, don't create two headers or footers (that is, A and B) when you are using the Every Page placement option. If you want to create multiple line headers or footers, you can do so within the Header A or Footer A window.

Viewing Headers and Footers

Note that once you close the header or footer window, the header or footer text is not visible in the document window. You can view a header or footer by selecting the Print Preview command.

Editing Headers and Footers

If you want to change a header or footer, you can do so by following these steps:

1. With the document displayed on the screen, choose the Page command on the Layout menu.

2. When the submenu appears, select the Headers or Footers command to display the Headers or Footers dialog box.

3. Select a header or footer option in the dialog box, then select the Edit button. The header or footer window appears. You can edit the text like any other text in the document window.

4. Select the Close button to return to the document window.

Hiding Headers and Footers

As you've already learned, headers appear on every page, odd pages, or even pages of a document. However, when a document contains a title page, you don't want the header and footer to print on it. You can hide, or suppress, headers and footers on the title page using the following steps.

1. With the document on your screen, move the cursor anywhere on page one of the document.

2. Select the Page command on the **L**ayout menu.

3. When the submenu appears, select Suppress. The Suppress dialog box, shown in Figure 18-4, appears.

4. In the dialog box, select the header you want to suppress (A or B), then select OK.

5. Select the Print Preview command to see that the header has been suppressed. When the document is printed, the header will not appear on the first page.

Lesson 19

Adding Page Numbers and Page Breaks

In this lesson, you'll learn how to add page numbers to a document, and control and insert page breaks when necessary.

Adding Automatic Page Numbers

In Lesson 18, you learned how to add page numbers to a document's header or footer text, but if you aren't using headers or footers, you can still have page numbers in a document. WordPerfect for Windows automatically numbers pages consecutively when you use the Page Numbering dialog box, shown in Figure 19-1. You can choose the position and the type of page number, and you can add accompanying text if you like. Here's how.

1. Move the cursor to the page where you want page numbering to begin.
2. Select the Page command on the Layout menu, then select the Page Numbering command. The Numbering dialog box appears.

3. Select the Position box to choose a page number position from the list. The sample pages above the box illustrate where the page numbers will appear when printed.

4. Select the Numbering Type box to choose a type other than Arabic numerals.

5. If you want text to accompany the page number, enter it in the Accompanying Text box.

6. If you want to force the current page to be odd- or even-numbered, select one of these options in the Force Current Page box, then select OK to return to the document window.

Page Numbering, or Header or Footer? The Numbering command has the following restrictions:

- up to 28 characters of accompanying text
- accompanying text on facing pages must be the same text
- no text enchancement (such as bold or italic) is available

When you want any of these features, use a header or footer instead.

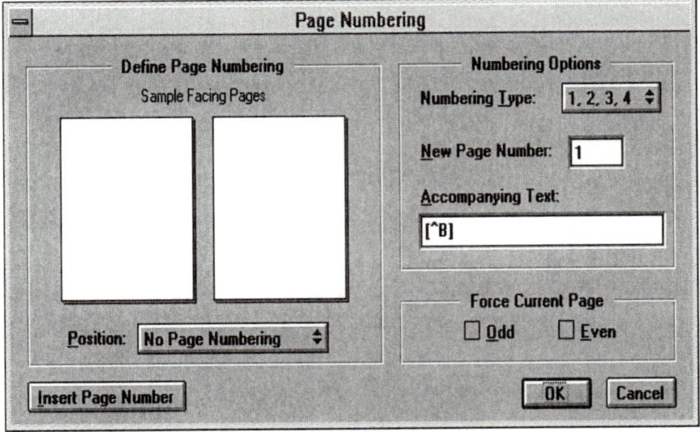

Figure 19-1 The Page Numbering dialog box.

When you add accompanying text, be sure to enter it in the appropriate place in the Accompanying Text box. For example, the box already contains the `[^B]` code for the page number; if you want the page numbers to read "Page 1," enter `Page` before the `[^B]` code. Don't forget to include the space following the word "Page." If you want the page numbers to read "- 1 -", enter a hyphen and a space before and after the `[^B]` code.

Viewing Page Numbers

The page numbers you enter using the Page Numbering dialog box aren't visible in the document window. You can view page numbers using the Print Preview command on the **F**ile menu, as shown in Figure 19-2. Automatic page numbers are printed on the first line (if you choose a top placement) or the last line (if you choose a bottom placement) of the text area. WordPerfect for Windows leaves one blank line between the page number and the body of the text.

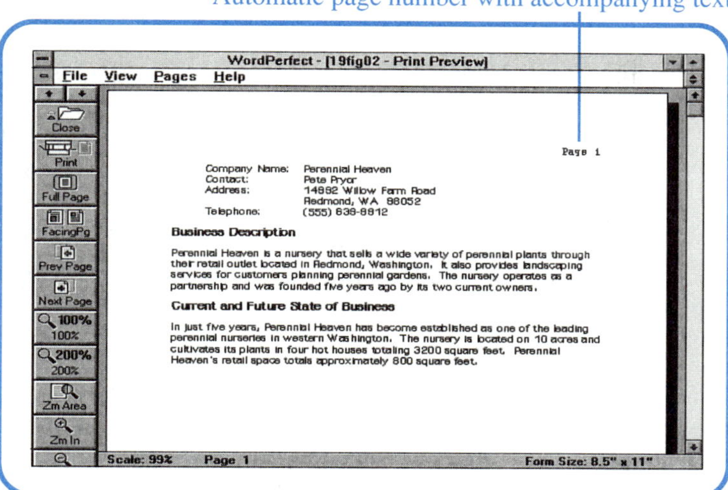

Figure 19-2 Automatic page numbers are visible using the Print Preview command.

Inserting Page Breaks

You don't have to worry about inserting page breaks in a document; WordPerfect for Windows does it for you. As you enter text, a *soft page break* is automatically entered in the document at the end of each page. WordPerfect for Windows knows where to insert page breaks based on the paper size and the margin settings you choose. Soft page breaks are visible in the document as a solid line extending horizontally across the document window.

Soft Page Breaks Soft page breaks are called soft because they may change positions, depending on the editing changes you make to the document. WordPerfect for Windows moves them to the appropriate place in the document. You can't move or delete a soft page break. *Hard page breaks* are called hard because WordPerfect for Windows *never* moves them. You insert them and you are the only one who can move or remove them from a document.

There may be times when you want to insert a hard page break in a document. For example, if your document contains a title page of only 25 lines, you would insert a hard page break after the last line to be sure that the subsequent text appears on the next page. To insert a hard page break, follow these steps:

1. Move the cursor to the point where you want the page break to occur.
2. Select the Page command on the **L**ayout menu, then select Page Break. WordPerfect for Windows inserts a double line that runs horizontally across the document window.

Shortcut In place of step 2 in the preceding steps, press Ctrl+Enter to insert a hard page break.

In this lesson, you learned how to add automatic page numbers to a document, and work with soft and hard page breaks. In the next lesson, you will learn how to find and correct spelling errors in a document, using WordPerfect for Windows' spelling checker.

Lesson 20

Checking Your Spelling

In this lesson, you'll learn how to use WordPerfect for Windows' spell checker to find misspelled words, capitalization errors, and duplicate words.

Using the Spell Checker

The spell checker in WordPerfect for Windows checks your document against a dictionary containing 115,000 words. When it finds a word in your document that doesn't match a word in the dictionary, it questions the spelling. To check spelling in the current document, follow these steps:

1. With the document displayed on the screen, move the cursor to the beginning of the document.

2. Select the Speller command on the **T**ools menu. The Speller dialog box, shown in Figure 20-1, appears.

3. Select the Start button. The Speller highlights the first unknown word in the document window. When the Suggestions option is checked in the Speller dialog box, all the possible replacement words are displayed in this box. Once the **S**peller is started, the S**t**art button changes to the **R**eplace button.

4. Select the correct word from the Suggestions box, or type the correct word in the Word box, then select the Replace button. The Speller replaces the misspelled word and highlights the next misspelled word.

5. Repeat step 4 until all words are corrected, then select the Close button to return to the document window.

6. Save your document.

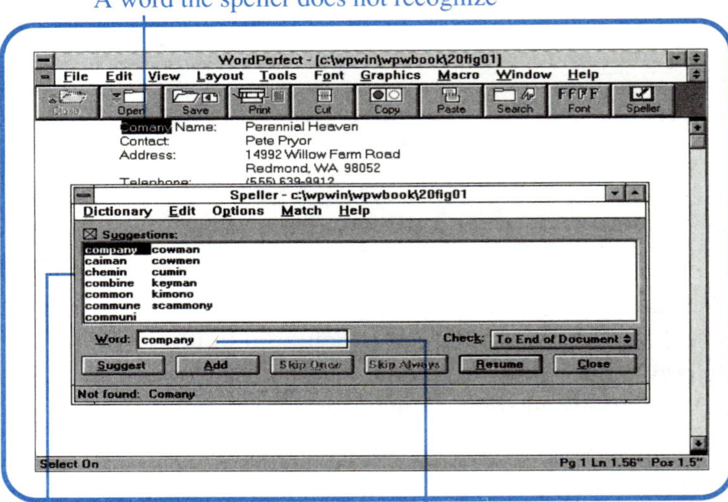

Figure 20-1 The Speller dialog box.

Speller Shortcut Open the Speller dialog box quickly by selecting the Speller button on the button bar or by pressing Ctrl+F1.

You can use the spell checker to check the spelling in headers and footers. Just open the header or footer window, then follow the steps just outlined.

Changing the Scope of the Spell Check

Now that you know how to use the spelling checker to do a simple check of a document, consider some of the choices you have. Notice, in Figure 20-1, the selection in the Check box is "to the end of document," which means the entire document will be checked when you select Start. By selecting the Check box, you can change the scope of the spell check to any of the options in the following list.

A word

The end of the document

The page

The end of the page

Selected text

The end of selection

The options that move to "the end of..." something, begin spell checking at the current cursor location. If text is already selected in your document at the time you select the Speller command, the Speller automatically checks the selected text only.

Quick Word Checks You can quickly check the spelling of a single word by selecting the word, then selecting the Speller button or pressing Ctrl+F1 to start the spelling checker.

Skipping a Word

There will be times when WordPerfect for Windows questions a word that is spelled correctly. This happens often with proper names and other common terms such as "Ave." or "St." because they aren't included in the dictionary. When this happens, you can click on the Skip Once or the Skip Always button. When you choose Skip Always, WordPerfect for Windows skips all future occurrences of the word in the document. When you choose Skip Once, WordPerfect for Windows skips only the current occurrence, but questions the word if it occurs again.

Adding a Word

Most business documents contain special terms such as product names, acronyms, or industry jargon. The speller always questions these words because they aren't in the dictionary. If you use special terms frequently, you can add them to the dictionary during a spell check operation by selecting the Add button. Once you add a word to the dictionary, it's treated like any other word—that is, WordPerfect for Windows will not question it again, either in the current document or in future documents, unless it's misspelled.

Speller Options

WordPerfect for Windows provides several options for spell checking a document. They are:

- Duplicate words
- Capitalization errors
- Words with numbers

The speller automatically checks for these occurrences unless you turn them off using the **Options** menu in the Speller window. To turn off these options, follow these steps:

1. Select the Speller command on the **T**ools menu, or select the Speller button on the Button Bar. WordPerfect displays the Speller dialog box shown in Figure 20-1.

2. Select the Options menu. Notice that all of the following settings are checked:

   Words with Numbers
   Duplicate Words
   Irregular Capitalization

3. To turn off one of these options, select the option. WordPerfect closes the menu.

4. To turn off additional options, repeat Steps 2 and 3.

5. Begin spell-checking your documents by selecting the Start button. Once you close the Speller dialog box, WordPerfect turns all three options back on.

When WordPerfect for Windows encounters two occurrences of a word in a row, the second occurrence is highlighted and the dialog box shown in Figure 20-2 appears. Choose Continue to keep both occurrences in the document, otherwise, choose Delete 2nd to delete the second occurrence of the word. If you want the speller to stop checking for duplicate words in the remainder of the document, check the Disable Checking box.

Figure 20-2 The Speller dialog box for duplicate words.

The speller checks for capitalization errors based on standard English rules for capitalization. For example, the speller would question *LEtter, lEtter,* and *leTter* if they appeared in your document.

When the speller encounters a capitalization error, the word is highlighted, and a dialog box appears. Choose Continue to leave the word as is. Choose Replace to have WordPerfect for Windows automatically correct the error based on standard English rules for capitalization. You can have WordPerfect for Windows ignore capitalization errors in the remainder of the document by selecting the Disable Checking box.

When a document contains words with numbers, such as a part number like BVUA291, Wordperfect for Windows questions it as a misspelled word, because BVUA291 doesn't appear in its dictionary. When a document contains many words like this, you can disable checking by selecting the Wrods with Numbers command on the Options menu.

Lesson 21

Improving Your Word Choice

In this lesson, you'll learn how to choose just the right words for your documents by using the WordPerfect for Windows built-in thesaurus.

Looking Up and Replacing a Word

When a document contains a word that doesn't quite convey the meaning you intended, or that has been used too frequently, you can use the WordPerfect for Windows Thesaurus tool to help you find just the right replacement word. For a selected word in a document, the thesaurus displays:

- Words with the same or similar meaning (*synonyms*).
- Different meanings of the same word.
- Words with the opposite meaning (*antonyms*).

To look up a word in the thesaurus, use the following steps.

1. Move the cursor to any character in the word you want to look up.

2. Select the **Thesaurus** command on the **Tools** menu. The Thesaurus window, shown in Figure 21-1, appears. The word you selected in step 1 appears as the heading (or *headword*) for column 1. Possible replacement words appear in the list box beneath it.

3. Scroll through the list box to view the replacement words. Select a word, then select the **Replace** button to replace the selected word in the document.

4. Select the **Close** button to return to the document window.

Shortcut You can open the Thesaurus dialog box quickly by pressing **Alt+F1**.

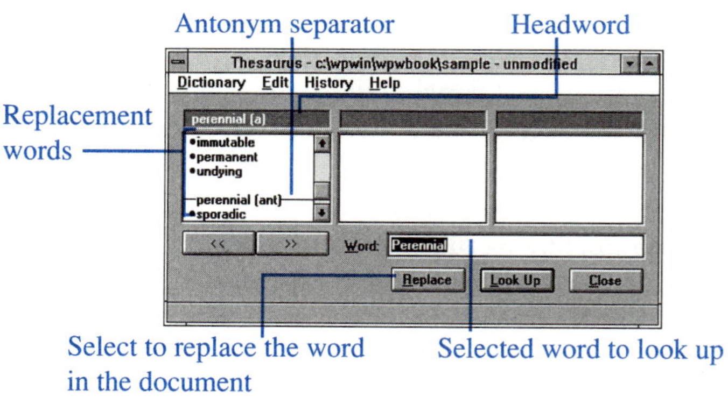

Figure 21-1 The Thesaurus window.

The word that you select to look up in the thesaurus is the headword and appears as the heading for the first column. Replacement words are grouped as nouns (`n`), verbs (`v`), adjectives (`a`), and antonyms (`ant`). They are separated by a horizontal line (see Figure 21-1). When the headword has more than one meaning, replacement words are grouped together by meaning into subgroups. Subgroups are separated by a blank line.

Doing a Thorough Search

When you do a simple look-up, replacement words appear only in the first column of the Thesaurus window. But sometimes the words displayed in the first column aren't quite what you're looking for. If a word seems to convey the right meaning but still isn't quite right, you can select any bulleted word in column 1 to become the headword in column 2. Here's how:

1. Move the cursor to any character in the word you want to look up.

2. Select the Thesaurus command on the **T**ools menu.

3. Select a bulleted word in column 1 and display a new list of words in the next column.

   Using the mouse:

   - Double-click on a word in column 1.

   Using the keyboard:

   - Select a bulleted word from column 1, using the up or down arrow, then press Enter.

   A *hand pointer* appears to the right of the word you selected (see Figure 21-2). Possible replacement words are listed below the headword.

4. If none of the words in column 2 seems right, you can continue your search by repeating the process in step 3. If you create more than three columns of words, move from column to column using the arrow buttons.

5. When you find the right word, select it, then select the Replace button.

6. To return to the document window, select the Close button.

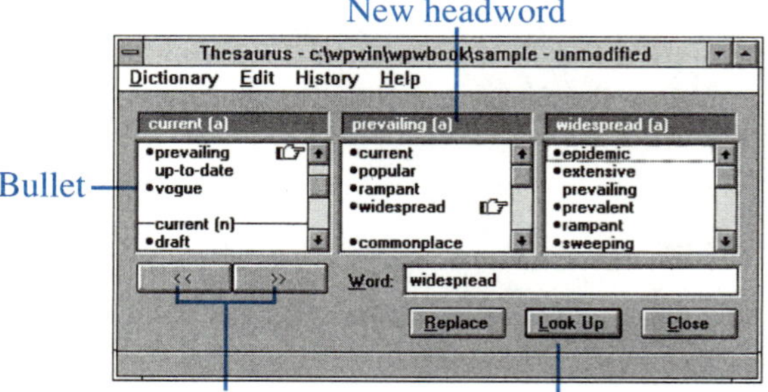

Figure 21-2 The Thesaurus window displaying three columns of replacement words.

Using the Look Up Button

At any time while you are using the thesaurus, you can use the Look Up button to look up a new word. Follow these steps.

1. Select the contents of the Word text box, then press Delete.

2. Type a new word to look up, then select the Look Up button. The word you type becomes the headword in column 1, and a new list of replacement words appears.

3. Repeat steps 1 and 2 to look up other words.

4. Select the Close button to return to the document window.

Retracing Your Steps

When you use the Look Up button, all headwords and replacement words displayed previously are cleared from the remaining columns. If you want to go back to a word you looked up before, follow these steps:

1. Select the History menu on the Thesaurus menu bar. The menu opens to display a list of all previous headwords since you started the thesaurus.

2. Select the word you want to redisplay. The word becomes the headword in column 1, and replacement words appear just below it.

3. Repeat steps 1 and 2 to redisplay other words from the History menu.

4. Choose the Close button to return to the document window.

In this lesson, you learned how to use the thesaurus to look up and replace words in a document. In Lesson 22, you will learn how to work more efficiently by opening more than one document at a time.

Lesson 22

Working with Multiple Documents

In this lesson, you'll learn how to open more than one document at a time, switch from one document to another, and display multiple documents on the screen at once. You'll also learn how to copy and move text from one document to another.

Opening More than One Document

One of the great advantages of WordPerfect for Windows programs is that you can open or create another file without closing the one you're currently working on. This can simplify your work tremendously, especially if you are copying or moving text from one document to another, or if you just need to refer to another document to work on the current one.

To open an existing document without closing the current document, follow these steps:

1. With a document open in the document window, select the **O**pen command on the **F**ile menu. The Open File dialog box appears.
2. Select a document to open, then select Open. The document you select replaces the previous document in

the current document window. The previous document isn't visible, but it is still open.

To create a new document without closing the current document, select the **N**ew command on the **F**ile menu. WordPerfect for Windows clears the document window and creates a new document with the temporary title `Document*` (where the asterisk is a number). You can use the **N**ew and **R**etrieve commands to open up to nine documents at once.

The Active Document When more than one document is open, only one is the active document. The title of the active document is always displayed in the Title bar.

Switching from One Document to Another

To switch from one open document to another, follow these steps:

1. Pull down the **W**indow menu. All open documents are listed in the bottom half of the menu (see Figure 22-1). The active document has a check mark beside the document name.
2. Select the document you want to switch to. Using the mouse, click on the document name. Using the keyboard, type the underlined number that appears to the left of the document name. The document you chose appears in the document window, but the previous document is still open.

3. Repeat step 2 to switch from document to document.

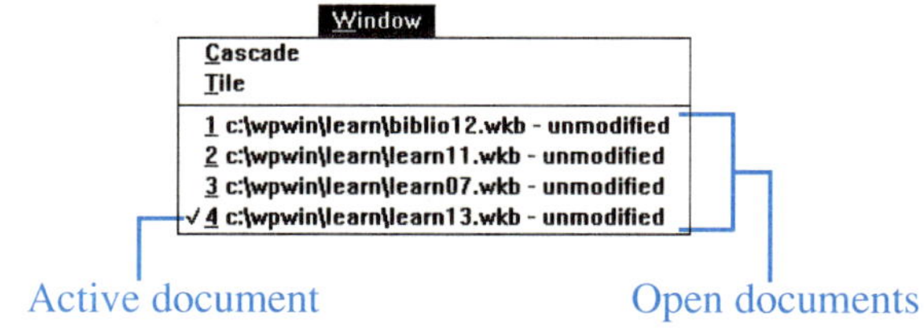

Figure 22-1 The Window menu listing all open documents.

Displaying All Open Documents

Rather than switching from document to document, sometimes it's more convenient to display multiple documents on the screen at once. There are two ways to do this:

- You can have WordPerfect for Windows arrange the document windows on-screen for you.
- You can size and arrange the windows.

WordPerfect for Windows gives you two arrangement choices: **T**ile and **C**ascade. When you choose the **T**ile option, the windows are arranged like tiles on the screen (see Figure 22-2). Using the **C**ascade option, the windows are overlaid on one another, with just the top and left edge of the lower windows visible (see Figure 22-3). To **T**ile or **C**ascade a window, select the Tile or Cascade option on the **W**indow menu.

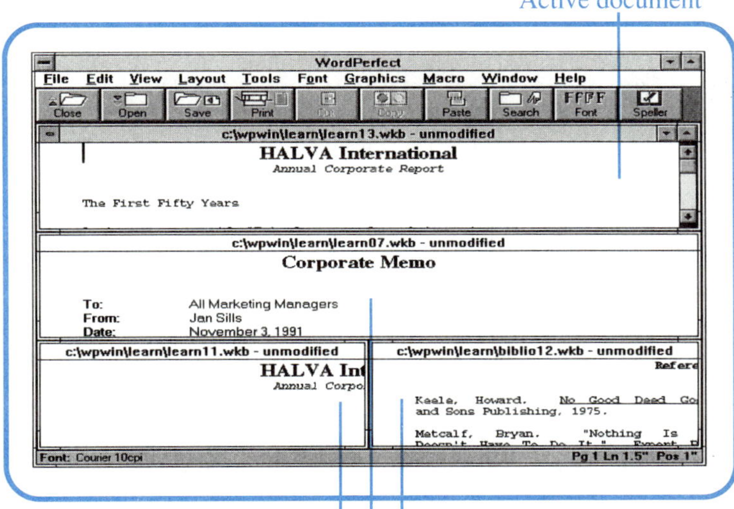

Figure 22-2 All open document windows are tiled.

The Active Window When multiple windows are displayed, the active window is the one in which the Title bar is highlighted. Your cursor only works in the active window. To work in another window, you must make it the active window.

Moving from Window to Window

When you display multiple documents on the screen, you need a way to move from one window to another. To move to another window using the mouse, follow these steps:

Click anywhere in the window that you want to be the active window. The Title bar is highlighted to indicate the new active window. (The cursor works only in the active window.)

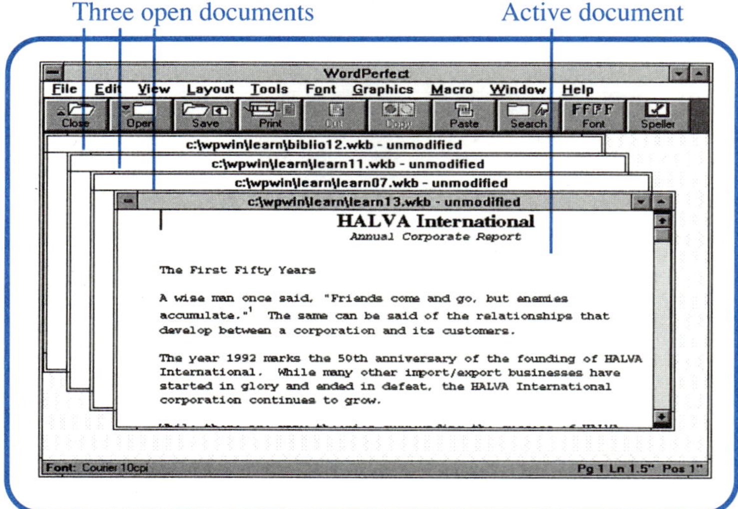

Figure 22-3 All open document windows are cascaded.

2. Repeat step 1 to move from one window to another.

To move to another window using the keyboard, follow these steps:

1. Press Ctrl+F6 to move from the active window to the next window.
2. Repeat step 1 until the Title bar of the window you want is highlighted. WordPerfect for Windows cycles through the open windows each time you press Ctrl+F6.

Arranging Document Windows Manually

When you use the **T**ile and **C**ascade options, WordPerfect for Windows automatically arranges all open documents.

Displaying 3 (or more) documents on-screen at once can sometimes make the documents more difficult to work with. Arranging the windows manually allows you to choose how and which windows to arrange, as shown in Figure 22-4. Follow these steps to arrange windows:

1. Move to the first window you don't want to display.

2. Reduce the window to an icon.

   Using the mouse:

   - Click on the minimize button.

   Using the keyboard:

   - Press Alt to access the Menu bar and then press the right or left arrow key until the document's Control Menu box is highlighted.

   - Press Enter, then choose Minimize from the Control menu.

3. Repeat step 3 for all windows you don't want to display.

4. Move and arrange the remaining windows on the screen however you choose. Using the mouse, click and drag any of the window borders to resize the window. Click on the Title bar and drag the window to move it to a new location. Using the keyboard, press Alt+Spacebar to open the Control Menu box. Use the Size and Move commands to resize and rearrange the remaining windows.

5. To restore windows reduced to an icon, double-click on the icon, or press Ctrl+F6 to move to the icon, then press Enter.

Closing a Window

When you no longer need to work on an open document, close the window using these steps:

1. Make the window the active window.
2. Double-click on the window's Control Menu box to open the Control Menu box, then select the Close command.

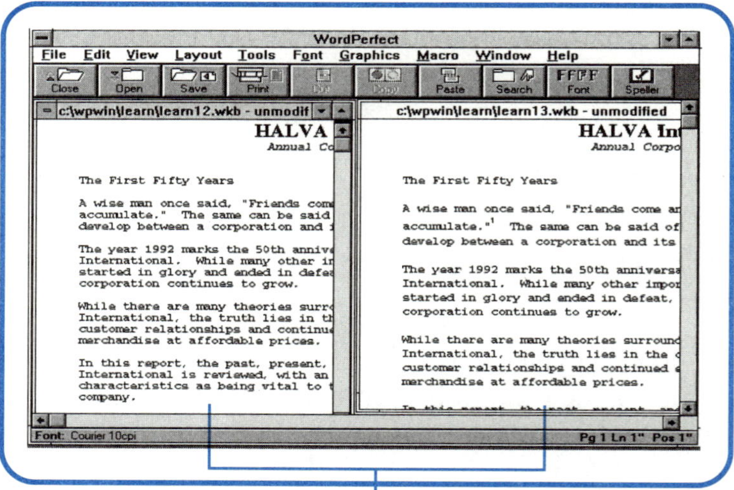

Figure 22-4 Two of five open document windows were arranged manually to suit the user's needs.

Click Close You can close the active window quickly by clicking on the Close button, or by pressing Ctrl+F4.

Copying Text Between Windows

To copy text from one window to another, follow these steps:

1. Open the document that contains the text you want to copy. Now open the document you want to copy text to. (You don't need to display both documents on the screen at once.)
2. Select the text you want to copy in the correct document.
3. Select the Copy command on the **E**dit menu, or select the Copy button.
4. Move to the other document and position the cursor where you want to copy the text.
5. Select the Paste command on the **E**dit menu, or select the Paste button.

Copy and Paste Shortcuts Press Ctrl+Insert in place of the **C**opy command and Shift+Insert in place of the **P**aste command.

Moving Text Between Windows

To move text from one window to another, follow these steps:

1. Open the document that contains the text you want to move. Now open the document you want to move the text to. (You don't need to display both documents on the screen at once.)

2. Select the text you want to move in the correct document.

3. Select the Cut command on the **E**dit menu, or select the Cut button. The text is removed from the document.

4. Move to the other document and position the cursor where you want to move the text.

5. Select the Paste command on the **E**dit menu, or select the Paste button.

Cut and Paste Shortcuts Press Shift+Delete in place of the Cu**t** command and Shift+Insert in place of the **P**aste command.

Lesson 23

Customizing the Button Bar

In this lesson, you'll learn how to edit an existing Button Bar, and create a new one suited to your individual needs.

Controlling Your Button Bar

In Lessons 1 and 8, you learned how to use the default Button Bar and the Print Preview Button Bar. WordPerfect for Windows provides these Button Bars to make selecting commands quick and easy. But, to be truly useful, Button Bars should contain buttons for the commands you use most often. WordPerfect for Windows allows you to create a button for any menu command. You can change or add buttons to existing Button Bars, and you can create your own Button Bars.

Editing the Default Button Bar

To edit the default Button Bar, follow these steps:

1. In the document window, select the Button Bar command on the View menu. The default Button Bar appears.

2. Select the Button Bar Setup command on the **V**iew menu. When the submenu appears, select the Edit command. The Edit Button Bar dialog box, shown in Figure 23-1, appears.

3. Follow the directions shown in the dialog box to add, move, or delete buttons. Notice when you move the mouse into the menu or Button Bar area, the mouse pointer changes to a *hand holding a button* (see Figure 23-1).

4. Select OK to confirm the changes and return to the document window.

When you add more buttons than can be displayed on the screen at once, WordPerfect for Windows adds left and right arrows at the left side of the Button Bar. Use these arrows to move to the left or right, along the Button Bar, when the button you want isn't visible.

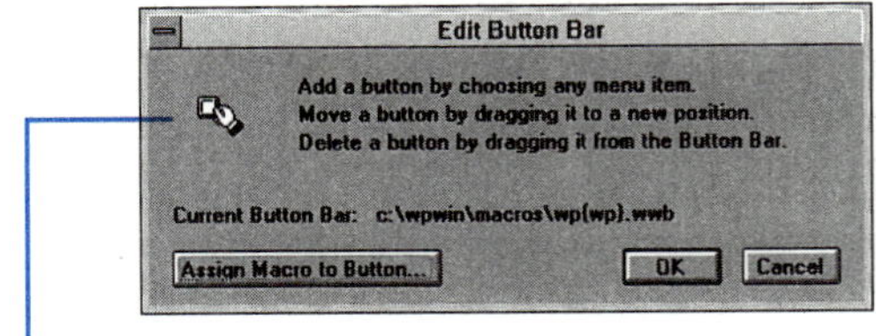

Figure 23-1 The Edit Button Bar dialog box.

You can use the steps just outlined to edit the Print Preview Button Bar as well. In place of step 1, select only the Print Preview command on the **F**ile menu, then follow steps 2-4.

Creating a Custom Button Bar

In addition to editing the default Button Bar, WordPerfect for Windows allows you to create your own Button Bar and save it separately from the default Button Bar. When you save a custom Button Bar, you can select it instead of the default Button Bar. To create a custom Button Bar, follow these steps.

1. If the Button Bar is displayed on the screen, select the Button Bar command on the View menu to remove it from the document window.

2. Select the Button Bar Setup command on the View menu. When the submenu appears, select the New command. The Edit Button Bar dialog box appears.

3. Follow the directions shown in the dialog box to add, move, or delete buttons. Notice when you move the mouse into the menu or Button Bar area, the mouse pointer changes to a hand holding a button.

4. When you have selected all the buttons for your custom Button Bar, select OK. The Save Button Bar dialog box, shown in Figure 23-2, appears.

5. If you want to save the Button Bar in a directory other than the current directory shown, select a directory from the Directories box.

6. In the Save As text box, enter a file name for the custom Button Bar, then select Save. WordPerfect for Windows saves your custom Button Bar and returns you to the document window.

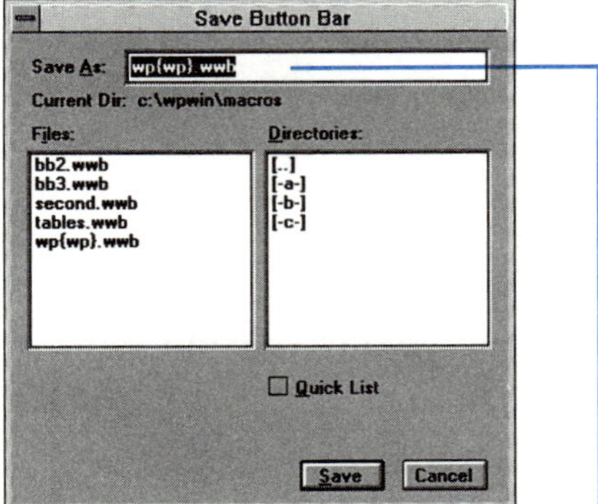

Enter a name for the button bar

Figure 23-2 The Save Button Bar dialog box.

Selecting a Button Bar

When you create one or more custom Button Bars, you need a way to choose the one you want to display. Follow these steps to select a Button Bar:

1. Select the Button Bar Setup command on the View menu. When the submenu appears, choose the Select command. The Select Button Bar dialog box appears. (Except for the name, this box is almost identical to the Save Button Bar dialog box shown in Figure 23-2.)

2. Select a Button Bar from the Files list, then choose the Select button. WordPerfect for Windows returns you to the document window and displays the Button Bar you chose in step 1.

Selecting a Button Bar If you change Button Bars frequently, try adding a button to each bar for the Button Bar Select command, so you can switch between Button Bars quickly.

Button Bar Options

WordPerfect for Windows offers several options for displaying a Button Bar. You can move it from the top of the window to the bottom, left, or right side of the window. You can also choose whether you want buttons displayed as text only, pictures only, or text and pictures. Follow these steps to choose the button position and style you want.

1. Select the Button Bar Setup command on the View menu. When the submenu appears, select the Options command. The Button Bar Options dialog box appears, shown in Figure 23-3.

2. Select a Position option and a Style option, then select OK. WordPerfect for Windows returns you to the document window, and redisplays the Button Bar based on your choices.

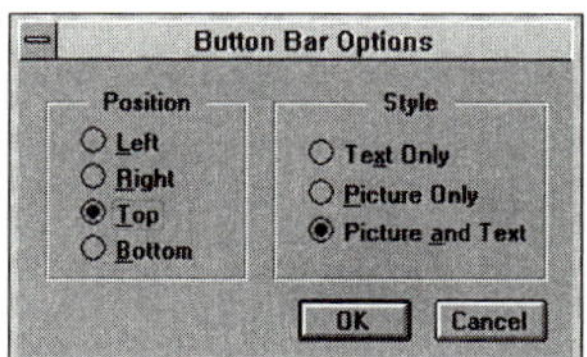

Figure 23-3 The Button Bar Options dialog box.

In this lesson, you learned how to modify the default Button Bar and how to create, save, and select your own Button Bars. In the next lesson, you will learn important techniques for managing your files using the WordPerfect for Windows built-in File Manager.

Overtime

Menu Options

WordPerfect for Windows offers ten pull-down menus located in the pull-down menu bar at the top of the screen. To pull down a menu, hold the Alt key and press the first letter of the menu's name, or click on the menu name with your mouse. The following sections describe the options on each menu.

The File Menu

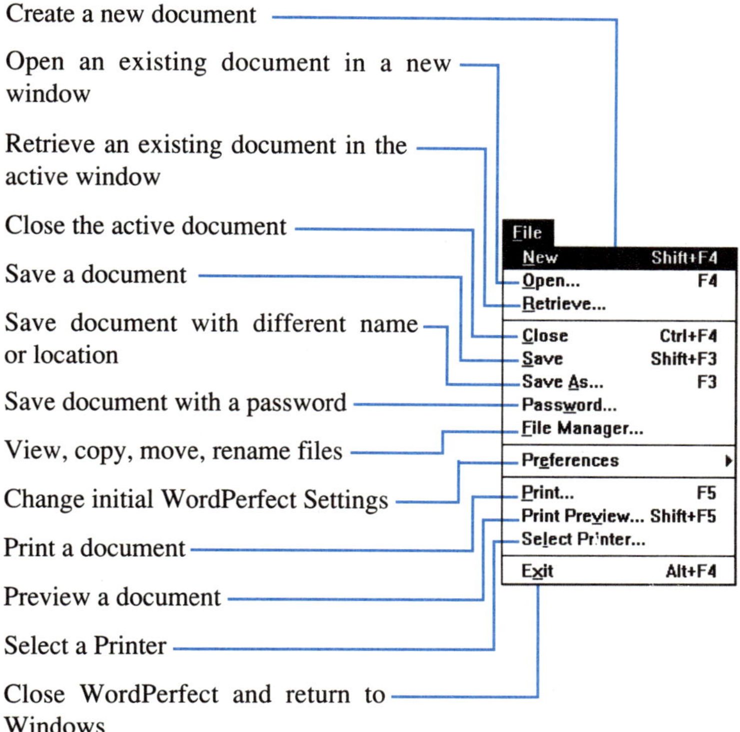

The Edit Menu

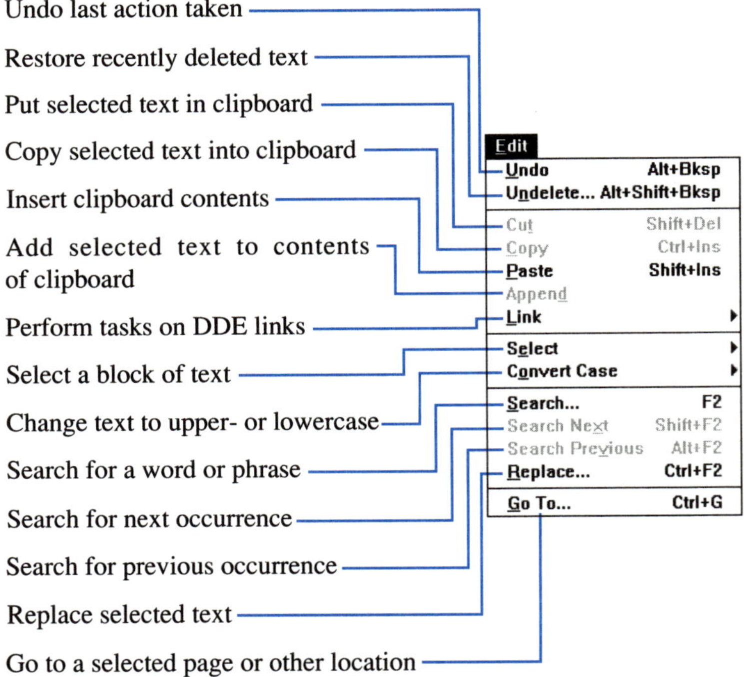

The View Menu

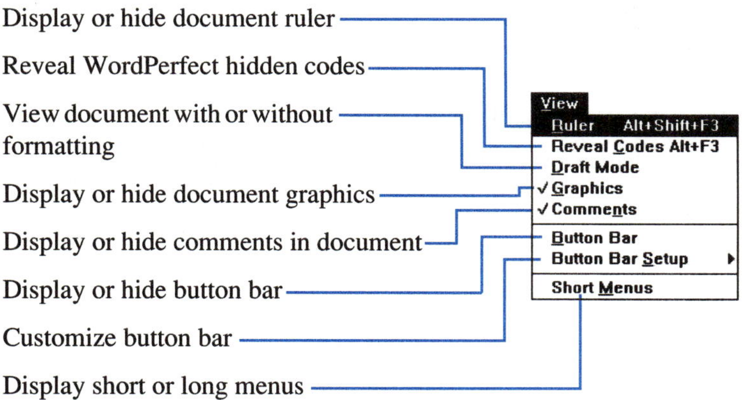

The Layout Menu

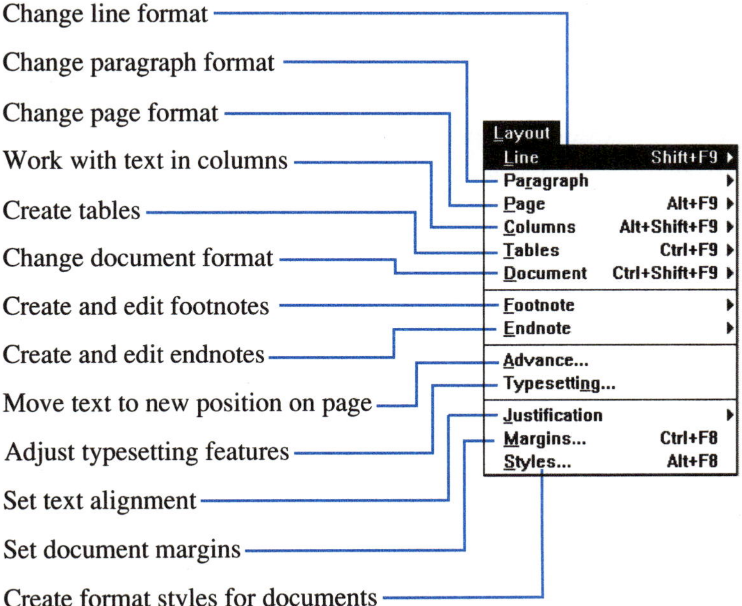

The Tools Menu

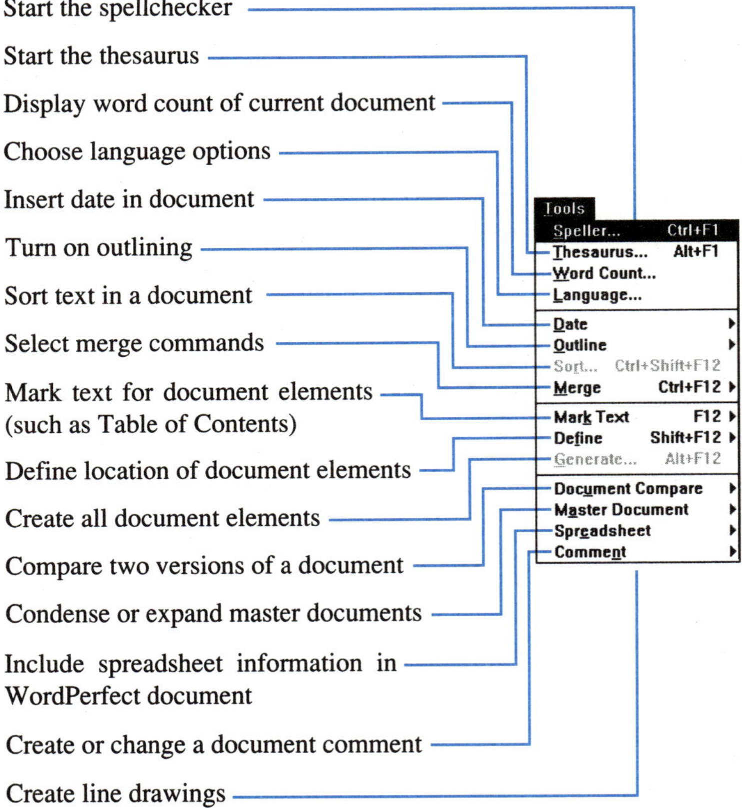

The Font Menu

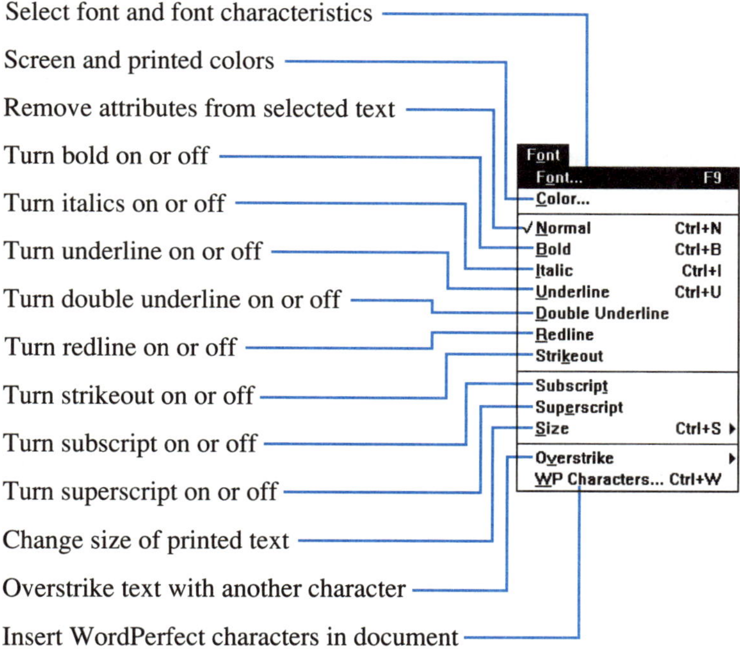

The Graph Menu

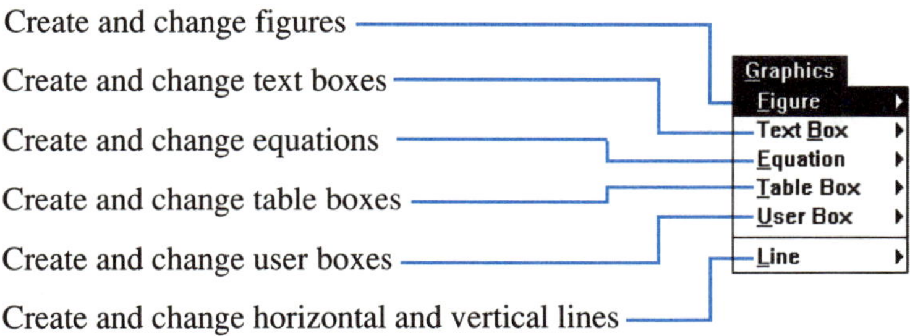

The Macro Menu

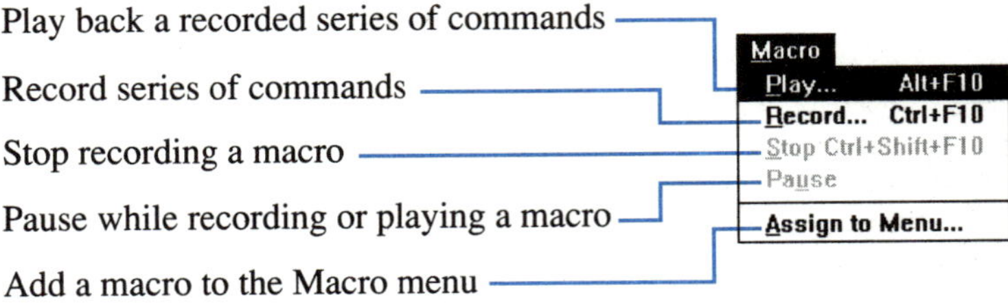

The Window Menu

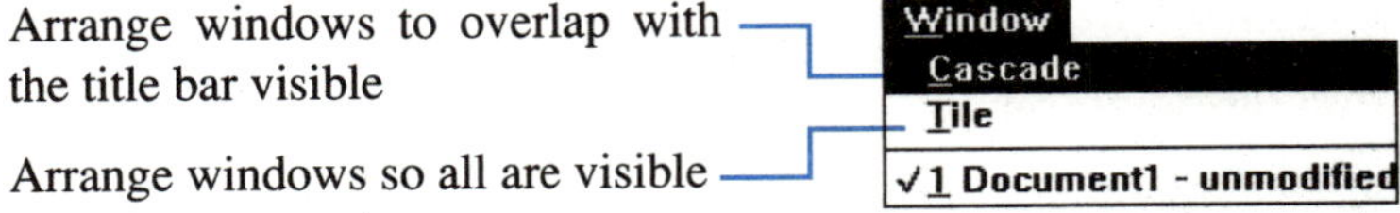

The Help Menu

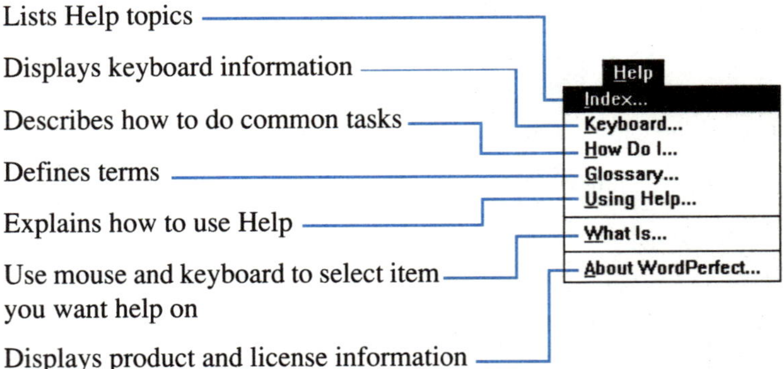

WordPerfect for Windows Formatting Codes

Following are the codes you see when you enter the reveal codes window in WordPerfect. These codes contain the document's formatting, as described earlier in this book.

Code	Meaning
[Bold Off]	Turns Bold off
[Bold On]	Turns Bold on
[Cntr Tab]	Center tab
[Dec Tab]	Decimal tab
[Dbl Indent]	Indents text from left and right margins
[Dbl Und Off]	Turns double underline off
[Dbl Und On]	Turns double underline on
[Footer]	Footer text
[Font]	New font
[Header]	Header text
[HPg]	Hard page break
[HRt]	Hard return
[Indent]	Indents text from left margin
[Indent] [Mar Rel]	Creates hanging indent

Code	Meaning
[Italic Off]	Turns italic off
[Italic On]	Turns italic on
[Just:Center]	Centers text
[Just:Full]	Aligns text left and right
[Just:Left]	Left-aligns text
[Just:Right]	Right-aligns text
[Outln Off]	Turns off outlined text
[Outln On]	Turns on outlined text
[Redln Off]	Turns off red text
[Redln On]	Turns on red text
[Rgt Tab]	Right-aligned tab
[Select]	Selected text
[Shadw Off]	Turns shadow text off
[Shadw On]	Turns shadow text on
[Sm Cap Off]	Turns small caps off
[Sm Cap On]	Turns small caps on
[SRt]	Soft return
[Stkout Off]	Turns strikeout off
[Stkout On]	Turns strikeout on
[Supress]	Supresses header or footer on first page
[Tab]	Tab
[Tab Set]	Set tab
[Und Off]	Turns Underline off
[Und On]	Turns Underline on

DOS and Windows Primer

This section explains the basics of DOS and some of the procedures you'll use when working with it.

DOS is your computer's *Disk Operating System.* It functions as a go-between program that lets the various components of your computer system talk with one another. Whenever you type anything using your keyboard, whenever you move your mouse, whenever you print a file, DOS interprets the commands and coordinates the task. The following sections explain how to run DOS on your computer, and how to use DOS to manage your disks, directories, and files.

Starting DOS

If you have a hard disk, DOS is probably already installed on the hard disk. When you turn on your computer, DOS automatically loads into your computer's electronic memory called *RAM* (Random-Access Memory). If you don't have a hard disk, however, you must insert the startup disk that contains the DOS program files into the floppy disk drive before starting your computer.

Working with Disks

The basic DOS commands deal with three elements: *disks, directories on the disk, and files in the directories*. In this section you'll learn the basic DOS commands for working with disks.

Changing Disk Drives

Once DOS is loaded, you should see a *prompt* (also known as the DOS prompt) on-screen that looks something like `A:>` or `A>`, (`C:>` or `B:>`) and tells you which disk drive is currently active. If you have a hard disk, the disk is usually labeled *C*. The floppy disk drives, the drives located on the front of your computer, are drives *A* and *B*. To activate a different drive:

1. Type the letter of the drive followed by a colon. For example, type `a:`.

2. Press Enter. The DOS prompt changes to show that the drive you selected is now active.

Formatting Floppy Disks

Before you can store files on a floppy disk, you must format the disk.

What is Formatting? The formatting procedure creates a map on the disk that later tells DOS where to find the information you stored on it.

Format Caution Be careful when formatting, because this procedure *erases* any existing information from the disk. Accidently formatting your hard disk will wipe out all program, system, and data files, so be careful.

1. Change to the drive and directory that contains your DOS files. For example, if your DOS files are in `C:\DOS`, type `cd\dos` at the `C>` prompt, and press Enter. For information on changing directories, skip ahead to the "Working with Directories" section.
2. Insert the blank floppy disk you want to format into floppy drive A or B.
3. Type `format a:` or `format b:` and press Enter. A message appears telling you to insert the disk (which you have already done).
4. Press Enter. DOS begins formatting the disk. When formatting is complete, DOS may display a message asking if you want to name the disk.
5. To name the disk, type a name (up to 11 characters) and press Enter. A message appears asking if you want to format another disk.
6. Type `Y` if you want to format additional disks, then repeat all steps. Otherwise, type `N` to quit.

Using DISKCOPY to Make Backups of Program Disks

Before you install any program on your hard disk or run it from your floppy drive, make *backup copies* of the original program disks, to avoid damaging the original disks.

When you use the *DISKCOPY* command to copy the program disks, you don't have to format the blank disks before you begin. However, the blank disks must match the program disks in number, size, and density or DISKCOPY will not work.

Protect the Disks Before using DISKCOPY, make sure the original program disks are write-protected. For 3.5" disks, slide the write-protect tab so you can see through the window. For 5.25" disks, apply a write-protect sticker over the write-protect notch. Many program disks are write-protected by the manufacturer.

1. Change to the drive and directory that contains the DOS DISKCOPY file. For example, if the file is in the `C:\DOS` directory, type `cd\dos` at the `C:>` prompt, and press Enter.

2. Type `diskcopy a: a:` or `diskcopy b: b:`, depending on which drive you're using to make the copies.

3. Press Enter. A message appears, telling you to insert the source diskette into the floppy drive.

4. Insert the original program disk you want to copy into the specified drive and press Enter. DOS copies as much of the disk into RAM as RAM can hold. A message appears telling you to insert the target diskette into the floppy drive.

5. Insert one of the blank disks into the floppy drive, and press Enter. DOS copies the information from RAM onto the blank disk.

6. Follow the on-screen prompts to swap disks until DOS displays a message asking if you want to copy another disk.

7. Remove the disk from the drive, and label it to match the name of the original program disk.

8. If you need to copy another program disk, press `Y` and go back to step 4. Continue until you copy all the original program disks.

9. When you're done copying disks, type `N` when asked if you want to copy another disk.

10. Put the original disks back in their box and store them in a safe place.

Working with Directories

Because hard disks hold much more information than floppy disks, hard disks are usually divided into directories. For example, when you install WordPerfect for Windows, the Installation program suggests that you copy the WordPerfect for Windows program files to directories called WPC and WPWIN on drive C. This directory then branches off from the root directory of drive C, keeping all the WordPerfect for Windows program files separate from all the other files on drive C. Directories can contain subdirectories as well.

The backslash (\) separates the names of the directories, giving DOS a path to follow in order to locate the directory at the end of the path. Use the backslash to separate all directories and subdirectories in a command line. A sample command line might look like this:

```
cd\forests\trees\maples
```

Changing to a Directory

Before you can work with the files in a given directory, you need to change to that directory.

1. Change to the drive that contains the directory.
2. Type `cd\directory`, where *directory* is the name of the directory you want to access. (For example, type `cd\nu`.)
3. Press Enter.

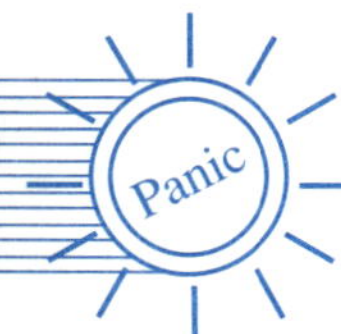

Displaying a Directory Name If you change to a directory that you know exists and the directory name does not appear in the DOS prompt, type prompt=pg and press Enter.

For more on working with directories and files, see the following section titled "Managing Directories and Files with the Windows File Manager."

Managing Directories and Files with the Windows File Manager

Windows is a *Graphical User Interface* (GUI) for DOS-based computers. Many users consider the Windows screen (interface) friendlier than the DOS prompt. Lesson 1, "Getting Started with WordPerfect for Windows" explains how to start Windows. Lesson 2, "Typing and Moving Around in the Text Area," contains a section that explains basic mouse techniques used in WordPerfect and Windows. Windows includes a program called the *File Manager* that allows you to work with disks, directories, and files.

The File Manager simplifies many of the file-related tasks traditionally implemented by DOS commands, including working with directories, formatting disks, and listing, copying, and deleting files. Most users find it easier to work with the icons and menus of the Windows File Manager than trying to remember the exact syntax needed to use traditional DOS commands. To open the File Manager, double-click on the File Manager icon in the Main Program Group.

Making Directories with the File Manager

The File Manager displays both a visual representation of your directory tree and a list of individual files in each directory. When the File Manager first starts, you are shown a tree with all the main directories branching off from the root directory of your current disk drive. You can change drives displayed by clicking on the appropriate drive icon. To make a new directory, follow these steps:

1. Pull down the File menu.

2. Select the Create Directory option.

3. Type the path and name of the new directory in the dialog box.

4. Close the dialog box by clicking on the OK button, or by pressing Enter.

Changing Directories

The File Manager displays a tree listing all directories branching off from the root directory. You can display subdirectories by clicking on any directory icon that shows a plus (+) sign. You can make any directory or subdirectory active by moving the mouse pointer to the directory name and clicking the mouse button. The active directory name is now highlighted.

Listing Files with the File Manager

To display the contents of any directory, follow these steps:

1. Highlight the appropriate directory or subdirectory.
2. Double-click on the directory icon.

Windows displays a directory window that lists all the files in the selected directory. You can display multiple directory windows on-screen simultaneously.

Copying Files

Copying files from one directory to another or from one disk to another is easy with Windows. To copy a file, follow these steps:

1. Select the file to copy in the directory window by placing the mouse pointer over the file name and clicking the mouse button. The file name is now highlighted.

2. To copy the file to another directory, pull-down the File menu and select Copy. The copy dialog box appears.

3. Type the new drive, directory, and file name in the To: text box. Select the Copy button, and Windows copies the file to the location you specified.

You can also copy the file to another disk by dropping the file icon onto one of the drive icons at the top of the directory file window. Make sure that if the target drive is a floppy drive, it contains a formatted floppy disk.

Deleting Files

To delete a file with the File Manager, follow these steps:

1. Select the file to delete in the directory window.

2. Pull down the File menu.

3. Click on the Delete option.

4. When the dialog box appears, click on the Delete button to delete the highlighted file, or on the Cancel button to cancel the delete operation.

Index

I

J-K

L

M-N

T

U-V

W-Y-Z